Cape Town Uncovered

Dennis Heyns

ISBN: 978 1496 06342 7

Cover Design; Dennis Percival Heyns
Graphic Design; Adrian Coetzer
Proof/Edit;; Esrelita Moses
DTP Typesetting: Trace Digital Services
Printing; Mega Digital

dennisheynsctu@gmail.co.za

For Julia and Jacqueline

Dedicated against Violence on Women and Children

Contents

Foreword

While writing this book, the further I delved into the dark side of human nature, the more I was drawn to the light – bringing me closer to God. I want the reader to go with me on a journey to people and places we know, but don't see or hear the truth about. I let people tell their stories. Some are horrific, others are sad but ultimately hope can always be found. The book may serve as a warning for some on how easy it is to choose the wrong path.

I was born in Cape Town, South Africa, and I think maybe that's why the Mother City is so close to my heart. I spent my school years in Durban followed by two years of National Service (compulsory for all white South African males over the age of seventeen during the apartheid years. We were conditioned by our government at the time to their way of thinking. If I knew then what I know now, then I'd rather have become a conscientious objector and gone to military prison.)

I returned to Cape Town after my military training and fell in love with the city all over again, first living in Sea Point, Clifton and then Camps Bay. The views are absolutely stunning around the Peninsula; I think Capetonians and tourists alike would agree. To me, Cape Town is not only the most beautiful city in the world, but it also has a spiritual presence. I wasn't wealthy but was very privileged and not aware of what was going on around me politically and otherwise

Maybe because of ignorance I never saw racism as a big issue, but Cape Town was what I'd call a 'grey' area during the apartheid years. In the turbulent eighties and even before then, whites and coloureds socialised together and seemed to get on fine.

7

There is a large coloured community in Cape Town. Coloureds account for about for about 10% of the country's population and are of mixed race. They generally are bilingual but some only speak Afrikaans. Some also switch to what is known as Kaapse Afrikaans (Cape Afrikaans – a dialect in Afrikaans, used predominantly by the coloured community in the Western Cape).

Their ancestry includes indigenous Xhosa people as well as European settlers and slaves from India, the Dutch East Indies, Malaysia, Indonesia, Mozambique, Madagascar, and various islands within the Indian Ocean. They were all classified as a single group–Coloured–under the apartheid regime. The first Afrikaans book was written in Arabic by an Imam (Muslim prayer leader) who was of slave descent. Coloureds are predominately found in the Western Cape and have a sense of humour like nothing I've ever experienced in the world. I always miss this when I travel abroad.

I lived in Scotland for almost twenty years and have two daughters there. After my divorce, I opted to stay there to be near my children until they were old enough. Once they were, I returned to South Africa and Cape Town.

I decided to investigate a different side of Cape Town while researching my book.

I met a tik addict who told me that he bought his drugs from gangsters in Woodstock and would introduce me to them. I met one of the senior members of the gang, told him what I was doing and asked if I could interview some members. He agreed and I was surprised at how keen everyone was to tell me their stories. I spent nine months doing research in this gangster's drug den where drugs were used and sold, almost losing my life at one stage.

I was then referred to Elepetra Ministries and Disciple school just outside Vredenburg on the West Coast, a rehab for reformed gangsters and addicts. Some were sent here by court order and others came here voluntarily. The rehab philosophy is based on replacing former addictions with the word of God. I spent a lot of time at Elepetra and got a lot more truth from former addicts and gangsters there. I spent many nights there, sleeping in the same dormitories, eating the same food and getting involved with their programme. I met incredible people and some of their stories really touched my heart. Some are included in this book and others I did not but their stories are as important.

I was warned by many that my life was in danger because some of the expose and the questions asked made me a target for a 'hit' by prisoners and the police.

I've never enjoyed anything as much in my life as I did writing this book. One day I'd be sailing with millionaires to Clifton sipping champagne, and the next day I would be in a drug den spending time with gangsters, rapists, and killers.

My parent's three sisters, two brothers and I grew up in Stamford hill in Durban. My first experience with 'gangsters' was when I was in primary school. The local park was called Sutton in our neighbourhood. I was ten when I ran into the Sutton park gang. The boys were all fifteen or sixteen but seemed much older. I was fearful of them as they had a fierce reputation – there were rumours of drug taking, beatings, stabbings and killings. Their main rivals were the Greyville gang who lived in the an adjoining neighbourhood, although there were many other gangs in other neighbourhoods. There was the Bluff gang, Durban North gang, South Beach gang, North Beach gang, Chatsworth gang and so on.

I was approached Brian Maxwell, by one of the older boys of the Sutton park gang when walking through the park one day. He was fierce looking and had a scar running from his mouth to his ear. I never asked and never found out how he got that scar. Brian wanted to know who I was and where I lived. I told him that my name was Dennis and I lived two roads from the park in Woodford Grove. He asked if I knew the Heyns sisters who lived in the same road. I told him that they were my sisters, a huge grin spread across his face and he said to me that if anyone ever gave me a hard time to come and see him and the same applied to my brothers and sisters. There were lots of rumours about Brian being involved in one fight or another but over the years I got to know him as one of the kindest and nicest men I've ever met. Brain turned to God and became a reborn Christian as a young adult and over the years it was always a pleasure when my brother Solly or I would bump into him. Sadly we lost Brian to cancer recently.

I soon learnt the rules of the 'gang', although it was more of a brotherhood than anything else. There was no induction, drug dealing, stabbings, beatings, robbing, killings or drug taking. Maybe one or two of the older boys smoked dope but this was frowned upon by everyone and as for gang fights, there were not any. But from time to time testosterone got the better of some of the boys and there would be fisticuffs amongst themselves or with other 'gangs' if they wandered into each other's neighbourhoods. The boys spent their time in the park playing football, swimming at the Sutton park pool and ogling girls.

I started spending more time in the park and often ran into the 'gang'. I befriended one of the younger boys called Derek Moore whose older brother Brian was also in the 'gang' One of the other boys was Peter Le Clos. We were all the same age. Peter had an older brother called Burt who seemed very scary to me at the time. His voice was deep and he had the same demeanor of mafia gang bosses I'd seen in movies. Burt never really hung out in the park but he became like a big brother.

Peter, Derek and I were inseparable, doing things boys did before television, computer games, mobile phones and gaming, which included climbing trees, playing football, fishing, building tree houses and camping. The only gaming we had was playing the pinball machine at the local shop run by an Indian family, with brothers Jay and Raj who also became good friends.

My brother Solly also hung out with us but he had his own

group of friends and often Peter, Derek and I would with our gang fight Solly and his gang which was nothing more than mud fights or breaking down each other's gang huts built in the field. But we'd do this for a couple of hours, get bored and then all go swimming together. Sometimes we would take along our much younger brother Jacques. Peter died suddenly from an undiscovered heart ailment when he was eighteen which was a shock to all.

Throughout our childhood the older boys always looked out for us and there was and still is an unspoken respect for them. When we moved out the neighbourhood and completed our National service, we'd bump into the local boys from time to time. Years later some had become successful businessmen, entrepreneurs – others got degrees in various fields becoming lawyers and magistrates. Burt's son Chad won a Olympic gold medal for swimming in 2012.

I thought that this was what gangsterism was, that in the end everyone's life turns out okay. How wrong I was.

I decided to do an investigative book on modern day gangsterism and people's life's affected by it.

I was looking to find the goodness in all this evil. I believe that most humans have a small part of God within them. The need for love and acceptance is a natural human trait, but rejection, hunger, pain and abuse in childhood creates the people some become.

I want the reader to see what drives people to do what they have to do for survival, no matter what the cost.

This account can be found in any big city in the world, Cape Town just happens to be where the investigation takes place. I want to show the reader a world that we rarely see or are aware of. We hear of the crimes but know very little of the circumstance behind it. We hear of the addicts but do not know their stories.

In South Africa there is little or no support system in place to support the poor, sick, hungry and destitute, or so I was told. Sometimes harsh decisions are made for survival. This is often the foundation for gangsterism in young boys.

I have met the people and here is their story.

Some have done it for greed and ego but for others it was circumstance. I have looked for the love in all this pain, suffering, violence and hate.

The methamphetamine-based drug 'tik' has swept into South Africa, becoming endemic to not only the big cities in South Africa but the smaller towns as well. It is at the heart of many problems.

Tik was virtually unknown in the country prior to 2002. It is known in other parts of the world as Crystal Meth but is called tik here. Tik is cheap, highly addictive and the user will often commit crimes to get the next fix.

Conducting interviews with drug users was often problematic. Firstly you did not know if they were telling the truth and at times I knew they were high and would talk total gibberish. I'd have to then on different occasions ask the same questions to see if I got the same responses.

I met two addicts who were known to inject tik. Jaun was a white man in his late twenties and you could clearly see that he was once a handsome man. He told me that he had Junior Springbok colours for swimming and while he still had muscle tone, he was at least thirty kilograms lighter. His face had aged from drug abuse and neglect and the remaining teeth in his mouth were blackened, he looked closer to forty. He started with dagga and then progressed to harder drugs, eventually injecting tik.

His girlfriend Anya was fifteen years older and often had outbreaks of pimples and herpes through bad diet, but would scrub up well before meeting a client, telling me there's nothing good make-up couldn't hide. She started smoking dagga as a teenager, also moving onto harder drugs like mandrax, ecstasy, cocaine, cat, heroin and tik. She also started hanging out with the infamous Hell's Angels. When she could no longer support her habit, she started selling her body, which she does to this day.

They asked if I wanted to watch them injecting. Jaun took out

12

a syringe and took some already prepared tik in liquid form from a vial. Tapping with his forefinger to remove any trapped air from the syringe, he then tied a belt around the top of his arm, pumped his fist a few times and inserted the needle into a vein in the centre of his arm. Once blood had seeped back into the syringe he slowly injected the tik, withdrew the needle and used a wad of cotton wool to stop any bleeding. He went quiet for a while, at which point Anya said: 'Sjoe he is so lucky to have such nice veins, I have to inject into my groin or jugular'.

She then went off on a rant, accusing me of knowing people I had no association with, and quizzing me on various brothels. We were interrupted when Jaun told us he'd injected too much tik. He went through the whole procedure again but this time injecting liquid valium into the other arm.

I could never get a proper story from Jaun and Anya and decided to pursue other avenues for interviews. I did however meet reformed gangsters and addicts and got their truth.

A former tik user who injected the drug for two years told me that he'd managed to beat the drug and stopped using but he still smoked marijuana and would dabble in whatever was available from time to time. The problem is if you are an addict, no matter what you take, you are an addict. And you will remain an addict until your dying day.

I also spent nine months with the 'Hard Livings Gang'. Their estimated numbers are between two and five thousand in the Western Cape alone. The majority are Cape 'coloured'. However, since the end of apartheid Blacks, Indians and whites are now members. They dress like British gangsters.

The Hard Livings gang is a street and organised group based mainly in Manenberg and Woodstock, Cape Town. It was formed in the early 90s by Rashied Staggie and his twin brother Rashaad. The gang started out as a street gang mostly involved in drug distribution for which they competed with a rival gang called The Americans.

After their distribution network grew, the Hard Livings gang, as well as the Americans, evolved into a structured criminal organisation involved in a wide range of criminal activities, including drug trafficking, weapon trafficking, prostitution, contract killing, extortion, diamond smuggling, robbery, fraud, money laundering, human trafficking and kidnapping. Known allies include the Sicilian Mafia, Nigerian Mafia and the Triads. The Hard Livings used to willingly remove their four top front teeth so that they could more easily be recognised.

During my time in Woodstock with a cell of the Hard Livings I had a few unusual experiences. I refer to this as 'The Complex'. It consists of what looks like a derelict house on entering. The rooms are sparsely furnished, floorboards in the main lounge area are missing and only a couple of old lazy boy chairs are present. The wall looks like a mixture of paint and dust.

Next to the main lounge area was a room with no windows and no lighting – it was furnished with an old couch and some broken chairs. I often saw people sitting in this area and I smelt Mandrax. It has a distinct chemical smell. I only assumed that they were using other drugs here as well.

Outside, towards the back, there was sewage water flowing out of a broken pipe and the whole area smelt of urine and human faeces. The backyard was filthy with rubbish strewn all over the place, which had no grass and was a mixture of mud and rubbish. Some underfed dogs were tied with ropes and some just wandered around looking for scraps of food.

Around the complex there are a number of makeshift shacks, crudely made of scrap wood and metal sheeting. Graffiti covered the walls, toddlers and young children were playing among the dirt. I saw people from all walks of life enter the complex – money and drugs changed hands, sold by men and women inside the complex. This is why we are called The Hard Livings, I was told.

I was talking with Azad, a senior member of the gang, one day when another member joined us. Mannie had just smoked some tik and apologised for being a bit out of it, he told me that the police had just searched him earlier as he is a known gangster. They would search him often, but would never find anything, he told me. Azad interjected and said he hides it in his safe. What safe would that be I asked. 'His safety deposit ass', replied Azad to which everyone burst out laughing. Mannie replied 'Yes and I am also carrying the 7inch knife which I inserted with my stash of four bags of tik earlier.'!

Another time I arrived in the middle of a police raid. (This happens on a regular basis) I had my writing bag and was neatly dressed, no one asked who I was or what I was doing there. I proceeded to one of the loft rooms to get a better view of events. The police arrested a man in a wheelchair as he had R2 000 in cash on him and 5 bags of tik worth R20 each. (R17 = 1 British pound or R10 = 1 United States Dollar) They left his wheelchair behind. I later asked Azad what the man's fate was. He told me that it happened often and that one of the members would go bail him out. Five minutes later I observed drugs and money changing hands.

One of the gangster girlfriends Desiree, who also lived in the complex, had an argument with her boyfriend the day before. He had gone out and not returned that evening. Desiree was distraught and also coming down from a tik and mandrax binge. She took 56 ecstasy pills of her boyfriend's stash. She is now brain-damaged, does not recognise anyone and no one is sure of what will eventually happen to her.

One Thursday afternoon, February 5th 2013, I was meeting with Azad when he told me that not only was it his birthday but that he just got married that morning. Azad was a Muslim and in Muslim culture men go to the mosque and get the blessing from the Imam without the women being present. On his return he informs his woman that they are now married. It was just a normal day and during that time a few of the men joined us and from time to time a women would come and wish him, there was no major celebration or party of any sort and everyone just went about their business like any other day. I was later told that the bride and groom had taken a substantial amount of drugs that evening.

I had some bad experiences during my time with the Gang. When I first started speaking to the Hard livings I had shoulder length hair. I cut it on 5th February, a day before my birthday. Later that month I was introduced to another one of the senior gang members who was high on drugs. He asked who I was and what I was doing there. I explained who I was but he just became more aggressive and said that he wanted proof of who I was because I could be anyone.

He started getting more agitated, saying that he wanted to see my driver's licence and proof that I was not a policeman. I have been in situations before when you know you are about to be attacked and here it was guaranteed with a weapon of some sort. Fortunately one of the other members stepped in and said that I was okay and could be trusted. I later heard that he was to be ranked again and had to draw blood, or worse, from an innocent. I did not interview this individual and avoided him during my visits to the complex.

The next incident involved the police. I was leaving The Complex one day and a young gangster whispered to me that the police were outside. I was not concerned as I knew people came here to buy drugs and I had nothing to worry about. As I walked outside there were two security vans (neighbourhood watch) and a police car. I heard someone calling out 'Umlungu' (white person). I ignored this as I knew what it meant. Knowing I was the only white person around, I also knew it was directed at me. Once again, I heard 'Umlungu'. I turned around and saw an African policeman in his police vehicle waving me over. I could see from his glazed eyes that he was high on something.

He said to me in an aggressive tone 'What are you doing here' I

16

explained that I was doing a story on the people in the complex and had been doing so for six months. He said to me 'How long have you been married'? This confused me at first. I replied that I was divorced, to which he replied 'Well you could not trust your wife but yet you trust these dogs!'

It was two weeks later when I arrived at The Complex late in the afternoon. I would always be there in the mornings before the gangsters got high on drink and drugs and also avoided spending time there over weekends. One of the gangsters asked for some money as his girlfriend was sick and they had no food. I handed him some cash (I later heard that the cause of her illness was that he had beaten his girlfriend and broken her leg in three places).

One of the gangster women waved me over. She asked me to sit down. I sat on an empty plastic milk crate and noticed three coins in a straight line on the floor in front of me. The woman had been drinking and could have taken drugs. I had interviewed her a few times and felt quite safe. She asked me why she should trust me and that some gang members were not sure about me.

I then noticed out the corner of my eye a gangster holding a hammer with a hanky wrapped around the handle standing behind me (if you are hit or stabbed blood has to flow onto the hanky as proof of the hit). I knew this was a hit on me and was looking for an escape route. If the coins were picked up the hit was to go ahead, I saw the woman shake her head at him and he walked away. They once again thought I was an undercover cop.

I was told by drug users that you become very paranoid when high and gangsters told me an innocent was always an easy target. I had become too complacent. I reminded myself that to them I was an outsider and any member would get rank if my blood was to flow. Fortunately my research was almost done at The Complex. I knew that I had to be very careful and would always let someone know when I entered and left from that day on.

I arrived at The Complex late one morning and started to

interview a senior gang member. I sat on a couch in his lounge which had no door. People were in and out of the room and it was a hive of activity. Gangsters were bringing in goods and money and drugs were changing hands. At one point a gangster came in and was given a removable taxi sign (one that attaches to the roof with magnets) my blood ran cold as I am aware that there are many pirate taxis in Cape Town, some use it to commit crime.

The previous day two girls were raped at gunpoint by a rogue taxi operator. The girls had taken the taxi late at night with friends who were dropped off first. The taxi driver told them that he had to make a quick detour whereupon he picked up some other men and raped the girls – only one of them went to the police. Robbery of passengers is also a common occurrence and most of these crimes go unreported.

I know this to be true because twenty years ago after leaving a venue late one night I jumped into a taxi parked outside. I always sit in the front and was the only passenger. We stopped at the next traffic lights and two men jumped in the back. One put a knife to my neck and told me not to make a sound.

I was driven to a deserted area of District Six and while still in the vehicle was stripped of my jacket and all valuables were taken from me. The men in the back seat found my bank card and asked me over and over for the pin number while hitting me. After some time one of the men in the back asked in Afrikaans 'Wat gaan ons nou met hom maak?' (What are we going to do with him now) – the driver replied 'Maak hom dood' (Kill him).I still could feel the cold steel of the blade pressing against my throat and knew that all it would take was one movement of the arm to cut my throat.

Somehow the knife was released and the two men in the back got out the vehicle and opened my door, I jumped out and stumbled as the knifeman tried to stab me. I got up and ran into the bushes nearby and did not stop until I reached the police station in central Cape Town.

The police were busy and said it would take a few hours before they could take a statement, so I just left. I went my girlfriend's house in Green Point. I explained what had happened. She said 'Oh My God your shirt is full of blood at the back, they must have stabbed you'. I took of my shirt and had no wounds. I can only assume that someone less fortunate had been in that seat before me.

The irony in all this was that here I was, twenty years later, interviewing the same kind of people that commit the same kind of crimes.

Most criminals will try and use you in one way or another once they gain your trust and confidence. I was asked by a gangster after meeting him once if I could go to court and tell the magistrate that he was of good character, after he'd been caught dealing drugs. Another gangster asked me if I could 'look after' some of his property in case it got stolen which was quite ironic as it was probably stolen in the first instance. I declined on both accounts.

Never be indebted to any criminal or gangster, even for a cigarette because sooner or later you will have to pay it back in one way or another. This is often the mistake made by first time prisoners – sex and violence is usually the payment.

I also spent some time with a former General of the 28s gang who is the only person to survive a death sentence when he left the number. His story is one of the most incredible and gives hope to others.

I conducted interviews in Drakenstein and Brandvlei prisons, initially asking the department of correctional services for interviews with pre-identified offenders. I was refused on the basis that I am media. I then arranged my own prison visits.

I interviewed the Anni Dewani killer at Brandvlei prison, Xolile Mngeni, who was sentenced to life for the fatal shot that killed Anni.

I visited PAGAD (People against Gangterism and Drugs)

19

Centre in Athlone Cape Town and conducted an interview with spokesperson Cassiem Parker. I contacted the South African Police Service for an application to conduct research within the SAPS. I went through the application process ending up at SAPS legal services – point eleven in the application states that a motivation for research indicating the extent to which the research will be in the interest of the service and / or the precautions to be taken, to ensure the SA Police Service is not portrayed in a negative light.

I was contacted by the Provincial head, but it was too late as I had gathered enough information, uncovering bribery and corruption in not only the police service, but also in the department of correctional services.

My trust in God made me not fear these people, but try and understand what made them who they became. Some had remorse and would change and were trying – and keeping in mind the only way out of a gang is with your life.

I was told by a member 'We are gangsters but we have the same needs as most people and have flaws. Ours are just worse than most'. Others were proud and spoke openly and freely about of their crimes of robbery, rape, violence and murder.

I found some stories funny, others made me sad and some made me very angry. I have heard many people say thank God this is not my son or my daughter. My reply to that is this could be your son or daughter so be warned! Yet in all of this I do not judge.

Please note this book is extremely graphic and depicts scenes of rape, murder, paedophilia, cannibalism, satanism and extreme violence.

I have altered names and, at times, location, to ensure confidentiality.

Illegal Drug Glossary

Most of these drugs are mentioned in the book and will give the reader a better understanding of how they are used, the effects and addiction potential.

CAT, Methcathinone (**α-methylamino-propiophenone** or ephedrine) is usually snorted but can be smoked, injected, or taken orally. The effects of CAT are similar to those of methamphetamine – including the inability to stop talking, both decreased and increased sexual drive and desire. Addiction potential 80%.

Cocaine, (**benzoylmethylecgonine**) is obtained from the leaves of the cocoa plant, also known as blow, coke, and nose candy. It is a white powder. Its effects can last from 15 – 30 minutes, to an hour, depending on the dosage and how it is taken. The drug can be snorted or injected. Effects include increased alertness, feelings of well-being and euphoria, energy and motor activity, feelings of competence and sexuality. Addiction potential 73%.

Crack, Crack cocaine is the freebase form of cocaine that can be smoked. It is also known as rock, work, hard, iron, cavy, base, or just crack; it is said to be the most addictive form of cocaine and is smoked through a small glass tube with a bulb at the base, it gives users an instant high with users immediately wanting more. Addiction potential 86%.

Dagga, also known as marijuana, ganja, weed, dope, smoke, is a relaxant. It is smoked in a pipe or joint and relaxes the user, it is also known to be used for medicinal purposes and is sometimes prescribed for cancer patients for pain relief. Addiction potential 21%.

Ecstasy, also known as 'E', is sold in pill form. It raises energy levels and has hallucinatory effects. The drug is known to heighten the sense of kindness, affection and loving feelings. Addiction potential 45%.

Heroin, also called H, smack, horse, brown, black and tar. Can be taken orally, injected, smoked, snorted. It is metabolically converted to morphine inside the body. Addiction potential 80%.

Mandrax, (methaqualone and antihistamine) also known as 'Buttons' is sold in a pill form. It is usually crushed and mixed with dagga and smoked in a dagga pipe or broken glass bottle neck or homemade pipe. It acts as a sedative and is extremely addictive. Also called a white pipe. It has a distinct chemical smell. Addiction potential 80%.

Tik, (methamphetamine in crystal form) also known as meth, ice, crystal. It can be snorted, smoked, taken orally or injected. It is odourless and usually smoked through a small glass tube called a lolly which has a bulb at the base. It gives the user an instant high. Users have reported losing a day or two of time. It creates a sexual appetite, insomnia and or lack of appetite. One hit can keep a user high for up to 8 hours. Users become very confrontational when coming down off a high and most will do anything to get their next high. Addiction potential 95%.

Whoonga (also known as Nyaope or wunga) is a street drug that has become widely used in South Africa since 2010. Whoonga contains classic psychoactive drugs like dagga, crystal meth or heroin, potentiated by interactions with ritonavir (an HIV drug). Whoonga contains efavirenz (alone or with the ingredients mentioned above), which supposedly has psychoactive side-effects. Addiction potential 80%.

The Numbers

26s — 27s — 28s

South Africa's prisons (inside and outside) are ruled by three numbers – the 26s, 27s and the 28s. Initially there were only the 27s and 28s. This is a brief introduction to that life.

The history of the numbers dates back many years, and started with a man named Po. Po was concerned why so many black men left their homesteads to go and work on the mines, never to return.

He went to meditate in a cave near a town called Pietermaritzburg in KwaZulu-Natal. One day he met a Zulu man called Nogoloza on his way to the mines looking for work. Po convinced him not to go and work for the white oppressors, but to join him instead.

Po eventually recruited 15 young men. He schooled them in a secret language – Sabela – and in the art of robbery. The men successfully robbed travellers and colonial outposts of their goods.

They split themselves into two groups – Kilikijan with his seven men who stole and committed their crimes by day and Nogoloza with his six men who committed their crimes at night. Po told the men to carve out their crimes on a nearby rock which served as a diary.

One day Po instructed that they buy a Rooiland (Red Earth) bull from a local farmer, who refused to sell it to them. They killed the farmer and stole the bull. That evening a big feast took place where the bull was slaughtered. Po instructed the two men to fill one of the bull's horns with blood and bile and to take a sip.

Kilikijan spat it out, claiming it would poison him. Nogoloza drank it without flinching. According to the members of Nogoloza this proved Kilikijan's cowardice, and Kilikijan members claimed that Nogoloza was an evil potion man.

Po then instructed the two men to impress the rules from the diary rock onto the hide of the Rooiland, thus giving each man a copy of the rules. Po explained that they must follow the rules as set out from the beginning.

Nogoloza received the hide and Kilikijan the rock. Both were instructed to carry the rules wherever they went. The rock was awkward to carry and was dropped accidently one day, rolling down a hill and splitting in two. This left Kilikijan's gang with half the rules.

One day the two gangs decided to embark on a joint raid. Nogoloza claimed to be ill and stayed behind. He asked for one of Kilikijan's gang members Magubane to also stay behind. On returning Kilikijan found Nogoloza engaging in homosexual acts with Magubane.

Nogoloza claimed that according to the hide this was allowed to avoid contact with women. Kilikijan claimed that Nogoloza added this rule to his hide after the other half of his rock had gone missing. The two had a huge fight and blood is spilled before Po arrived to intervene.

Po then sent Kilikijan to the mines to see if men there were engaging in homosexual acts and in doing so discovers this to be true. However opinions remained divided on whether homosexual acts were justified.

A final decision on whether sexual intercourse between men was allowed never came to pass, as Po died before he could do so.

The two gangs then went their separate ways. Nogoloza now had eight men, including Magubane. Kilikijan had seven men.

It is said this is where the numbers 27s and 28s originated from – the 2s being the two leaders. The 28s emblem is the Zulu shield. The skin is made from the legendary Rooiland cow's remains.

After some time both men ended up in prison in Durban, where they encountered a group of six men who were controlled by a man called Grey. The men would sit in a circle of six and flip a silver coin between them. Nogoloza demanded that the men to hand over their belonging. They refused. Kilikijan told Nogoloza that the men were skilled smugglers and gamblers. Nogoloza decided to call the coin 'Spyker' (nail) while Kilikijan wanted to call it 'Kroon' (crown). A fight broke out between the two as Nogoloza wanted to use the gamblers for sex.

After a lot of deliberation Nogoloza decided to call the group the 26s.This number was to represent their inferior status. Nongoloza also informed Kilkijan that he and his men would have to answer for the actions of the 26s. It was said that Nongoloza said to Kilkijan 'When they commit a wrong, I will not go to them, I will come to you'. Kilkijan replied 'That is all well and good, but when you wrong them I will come to you.'

Finally the three camps were formed. The 26s were responsible for gambling, smuggling and accruing wealth in general. The 28s were the warriors and responsible for fighting on behalf of all three groups, and the 27s were the guardians of gang law and the peace keepers between all the gangs.

Then there are the Franse who are not gang-affiliated and are the target of all the numbers in all the camps unless you are a numbers Frans. If that's the case, then you are protected by that number. There is 'ligte werk' (light work) or harde werk (hard work). If you are a hard working Frans you are just below a soldier, you carry their knives money and drugs.

The light work is for the weaker Franse who become 'wyfies' and are used as women. These Franse usually get taken by the higher ranks in the gang and these 'wyfies' get preferential treatment in their cell. You have to work up in the ranks before you can take a 'wyfie'.

The wyfie Franse get rationed with eight cigarettes a day and can help themselves to food in the numbers locker, they get jam and meat for their bread and access to drugs. They get to shower first and make themselves nice for their men's sexual demands, usually at bedtime. If you get beaten as a Frans and your head is cut, you may not join any number as you are now a 'vuilgat' (dirty ass).

New rules and a strict code of conduct were drawn up. It was decided that when a gangster broke a rule, the blood of a warder or Frans must be spilled to set things straight.

There were also the 24s, known as the 'Air Force' and their biggest ambition in prison is to try and escape at any time. They have been known to work with the 28s. The 28s would start a fight or sanction a hit, creating a diversion which would in turn give the 24s an opportunity to escape. In return, when any member of the 'Air Force' was sent to prison they had to smuggle in contraband.

The 25s, known as 'The Big Fives' are predominately found in the former Free State prisons. The 29s are known as 'The Desperados' – both these gangs are known to have been police and prison informants. They were often the target of the 26s, 27s and 28s. The 24s 25s and 29s are known to have disbanded and integrated into other prison gangs.

The 26s are called Sonop (sun up) as they do their work during day, the 28s are called Son af (sundown), they work by night and the 27s are called Hollanders (Dutchmen) – they work day and night.

There are two structures in the 28s prison gangs. (The number 1s and the number 2s). It is run like a military operation with ranking tattooed on the skin.

Number 1's;
Government (Makwezie)
General Six and Six stars = Twelve
Inspector Four and Four stars = Eight
Doctor Six and Six stars = Twelve
Maballaan Four and Four Stars = Eight
Advocate Two and Two stars = Four
Magistrate Three and Three stars = Six
Judge Six and Six stars = Twelve
Captain Two and Two = Four

Number 2's;
General Six and Six stars = Twelve
Inspector Four and Four stars = Eight
Doctor Six and Six stars = Twelve
Maballaan Four and Four Stars = Eight
Advocate Two and Two stars = Four
Magistrate Three and Three stars = Six
Judge Six and Six stars = Twelve
Captain Two and Two stripes = Four stripes in total
Sergeant Major Three and Three stripes = Six
Sergeant 1 One and One stripes = Two stripes and a star on the forehead.
Sergeant 2 One and One stripe
Guard No ranking
Soldier No ranking

The 26s salute:
Consists of a raised thumb

The 27s salute:
Consists of a thumb and the index finger

The 28s salute:
Consists of the thumb and the first two fingers

South Africa has eleven official languages. The numbers are taught a secret language called Sabela in prison when joining. During the initiation stage of a new recruit, they must learn the values and history; the gang will inform the new recruit on gang tradition and policies. These policies play an important role and if any member ever forgets the policies, they will be severely punished.

Numbers execute their hits and major decisions according to the date of the month. A 26 will use the 26th of the month, a 27 will use the 27th, and a 28 the 28th of a month.

There is only one way to leave the number once you have been stamped (tattooed) and that is with your life.

The Home Boys

Blood in Blood Out

The first time Azad was introduced to me I could see he was a gangster by his prison tattoos. He has a teardrop under his eye and after gaining his confidence, I asked him what it was for. He told me that it meant he would cry no more and fear no more. This is his story …

I was five years old and remember living in my granny's house in Manenberg with my four brothers, two sisters, an aunt and uncle, as well as our cousins – in a three bedroom house. At this point my mother was in prison for theft. I did not know my father until much later in life.

Life was hard as there was little or no food at times, at times a generous neighbour used to bring a food parcel, but my cousins always got there first and left very little for us. In the winter we were freezing and in summer boiling hot. We often used to take our blankets and sleep outside in the summer. I started stealing sweets and food at the local shop at the age of six. I stayed there for three years before I was sent to the orphanage.

Life at the orphanage was great; I had my own bed, got food three times a day, played sports and went on camping trips. My mother managed to get a house on her release from prison and I'd go and live with her on weekends and holidays.

My older brothers had joined the Hard Livings Gang and I couldn't wait to join the ranks. They always had money. Even at the age of ten I knew that money meant freedom. I ran away from the orphanage, and did so several times, but each time they'd fetch me and take me back. After a while they just left me alone and, if any, this is the one regret I have in my life.

I started smoking at the age of eleven and started to pickpocket, steal bicycles and used to run drugs for my brothers. Soon I was looking forward to my weekends at home, even if my mother was high on drink and drugs with no food to eat. I started sniffing glue and thinners. One day my brothers told me I was ready to join the gang. I was given a knife and instructed to stab a member of the Naughty Boys gang.

After smoking some mandrax and drinking a half a bottle of wine I went with two other members of the HLs to Cape Town city centre and to the area where the Naughty Boys used to hang out. It was winter and getting dark early. It must have been eight pm.

We went to Cadiz, a 24-hour take away on Long Street and saw one of the Naughty Boys standing outside the shop. I walked up to the boy who was about fourteen and asked for a light. As he reached into his pocket I pulled out the knife and stabbed him in the face. There was blood everywhere and adrenaline was now pumping through my veins, giving me a high that made me fearless. The boy bent over clutching his face and I stabbed him another three times in the back as he fell to the ground.

I ran away and on the train met the two HLs. They were congratulating me and said how proud they were of me and that we were now all family. I first had to take the standard beating by the gang and then we had a party till the early hours of the next morning. For the first time in my life I felt respected and part of a brotherhood.

I used to climb through the train window when it pulled into a station to avoid paying a fare. One day as the train was leaving the station I saw another boy trying to climb through the window. I went over and pulled him inside. This the day that I met Damien

AKA Die Duiwel (The Devil), from that day we became great friends.

Following my conversation with Azaad I was introduced to Damien in a drug den also known as The Complex in Woodstock, Cape Town. This is his life story ...

My name is Boy AKA Die Duiwel (The Devil). When I was three my dad went to prison for murder. We moved to Parkwood, a virtual gangster's paradise. My mother was pregnant with my sister. We lived well until my stepfather came on the scene. The people in the neighbourhood now all disliked us because our stepfather Japie was selling Mandrax.

He beat us regularly. I was five years old. I became rebellious and would sleep under a Bakkie (4x4 vehicle) in the front of the house. I was stealing chocolates and sweets from the local shop. I got caught a few times and got a beating which I now was becoming used to. My mother was concerned for my wellbeing and sent me to a place of safety. Not long after, I ended up in reformatory.

At the age of seven I joined the Cape Town Scorpions gang. I was in a reformatory called Bonnytown. I was given a knife with a hanky wrapped around the base, and I stabbed a member of the Born Free's in the eye. Then I was sent to a children's home in Tulbagh. Here I was taught how to play rugby, box and swim. I loved it there. I was young and missed love. I ran away a few times and was then sent to a reformatory in Atlantis where it was much harder. This was a trade school and I was taught plumbing. I kept on fighting and was now ten years old. Several of the bigger boys had tried to sodomise me but could not because I was a fighter. I started raping the weaker kids and this was and is the only love I know and I take it when I want.

I was placed with a family in Tableview at age eleven. A fellow member of the Cape Town Scorpions asked if I wanted to join the Hard Livings, which I said I did.

I was summoned to a meeting with some senior gang members.

33

They put a dagga (marijuana) pipe, a knife and money in front of me and said I had to choose one (find out if chose money or pipe) I chose the knife and was instructed to stab one of the Junkie Funky Kids. I did this with pleasure. Then I was given a beating by thirteen men on the one side and thirteen on the other – I was in the middle. It was a test to see if I could take the pain. I did not scream and proved to be a man, and became one of the Hard Livings.

A few months later I was asked to stab a member of Die Rotte, (The Rats) a rival gang. I stabbed the man but he managed to stab me in the arm. I was given a rank of two lines (a young captain). Then we retaliated and had a gang fight with twenty other members of Die Rotte. We beat them and they ran a way but we cornered one and we all stabbed him to death. Some of us were arrested but my case got thrown out of court because I was a juvenile.

We used to travel to Cape Town on the train and rob commuters, threatening them with a range of weapons anything from a knife, axe or panga (a panga is very similar to a machete and is used to chop down sugar cane at the plantations). We use to buy drugs with our proceeds.

I was sent back to school in Atlantis, but I was still rebellious. I used to look up the teachers dresses and let the class know what colour panties they were wearing that day. I was stealing, using drugs and raping lots of boys at school, nobody ever said anything out of shame and the fear of my wrath. I beat and stabbed people before robbing them.

I was sent to Porters school which was known as Klein Pollsmoor (Small Pollsmoor Prison).I was now twelve years old.

There were two men in my cell called Popeye and Pretty Boy. One evening they both grabbed me and tried to rape me, I started shouting and some 26s and 28s heard me. They told to me pull the blanket over my head and accept my fate. I shouted no, they would kill me. Then Pretty Boy and Popeye started beating me with Die Beker. (The Cup, a steel cup that is issued to all prisoners

34

to drink out of). I knew that if they cut my head with the rim of Die Beker that I would be a Vuilgat (dirty ass) and would not be able to join any of the numbers. I just covered my head and took the punishment, they did not rape me. (All steel has since been replaced by plastic, but prisoners always find a way to make a weapon I was told).

The 28s approached me and said that Die Glass (The Binoculars) had been watching me and did I want to join their number. I said I did and was then instructed to attack a Frans (someone with no gang affiliation).

It was a Monday and I waited until after the evening meal, then beat up a Frans who had just been assigned to our cell that day. I managed to cut his head and knew that he would not be able to join a gang and would have a very hard time in prison from then on. The prison officers took me out the cell and beat me nearly to death with their batons. I was returned to my cell but even though I could hardly move and was in pain, I felt a sense of achievement and pride. I was to be initiated into the 28s the next Sunday but unfortunately I was transferred back to Tokai reformatory.

I was released after nine months of awaiting trial as the docket was missing. I caught a train from Salt River and had no money. I was trying to climb through the window when I felt someone pull me up. This is when I met Azad. We became great friends and started robbing together. Azad was also an HL and when you are a fellow gang member you do not ask too many questions. We were stoned, drunk and high most of the time before, during and after we would commit a crime. I was now fourteen.

One Saturday afternoon after knowing Azad for about three months I was invited to a birthday party at his mother's house. I was surprised to find that both our parents lived in the same street. I only heard of other HLs living here but never bothered to ask who they were.

Now we started spending more time with other HLs and we also had a gang hut in Mitchell's Plain, where we would meet before and after crimes. This is also where we would gang rape girls.

We had a big table in the centre of the room. We used to give a young girl some drugs to lure her to the hut, strip her naked, spread eagle her on the table and take turns having sex with her. Sometimes there were up to thirteen men. This was known as Die Tafel (The Table). It wasn't long before I was sent back to Tokai reformatory for robbing a liquor store at knifepoint.

I got word that an officer was needed in the HLs and was asked if I was interested. I agreed. One of the teachers, Mr van der Merwe, was a teacher I didn't like at all. One day he started shouting at me and saying that I was a no good gangster and that not only would I amount to nothing in life, but I'd probably spend most of my life in prison. I stabbed him three times in the classroom in front of the other pupils. I was sent to Wynberg Magistrate's Court and sentenced to six of the best lashes with a cane.

A wet cloth soaked in salt was placed on my naked bottom. I was then hit with such force that it broke the skin in some places and when the salt soaked in, it was excruciating. Thereafter I was put in the cells for 28 days.

I was now eighteen and six months.

One evening Azad and few of the other members and I were driving around Cape Town. We were high on drugs when we saw a couple of tourists leave a restaurant. We pretended to be lost and I got out of the car and asked for directions. They said they were on holiday from Europe and did not know the area. I pulled out an axe and told them to get in the car. The woman started sobbing and I smacked her in the face, telling her to shut up if she didn't want to get killed. There was another car full of members behind us and we signalled to them to follow us. We drove to an abandoned car park and robbed and raped them both. We never got caught.

Azad and I now started housebreaking. We would get some of our women to go get work in affluent areas as housemaids. They'd tell us about valuables, alarms and what the obstacles were. We knew when the homeowners were out so this was easy pickings. Sometimes they took Polaroid photos of the interior and we could then steal on order.

I met a girl called Precious on the train one day and soon we were living together. She knew what I was and what I did for a living but did not care. Precious's father was a doctor and mother a lawyer. She was raised in a very conservative family but thrived on the dangerous man that I was. She fell pregnant a few months later to her family's disappointment. We were sleeping in my mother's house when at four one morning seven policemen burst into the house and arrested me.

I was charged with Azad on several counts of housebreaking. One of the girls that worked the houses for us got caught with twenty bags of tik and instead of doing jail time informed on us. We both got eighteen months jail time.

In prison Azad wanted to join the 26s but I convinced him to become a 28. We both beat a Frans with Die Beker. We took the usual punishment of beatings by the prison officers and thereafter were inducted into the way of the 28s.We started to receive military training of the 28s and rules.

We both got released after nine months but I was back after two weeks for attempted murder and robbery. I hit a man over the head with an axe because he would not hand over his money. I got two to four years prison time.

I was sent to Klein Drakenstein prison which was where I met Imran AKA the Enforcer, who turned out to be Azad's older brother. We were both 28s. This was a very bad prison and there were many murders. During my time here between 15 and 20 inmates were killed. One year after my sentence I was released on amnesty by FW De Klerk. I was back in prison three months later for attempted murder and robbery again. I got five years prison time in Pollsmoor prison.

I was in medium B section and was constantly harassed by a prison officer named Danie Vermaak. One day I spat in his face, I was severely beaten by four officers.

A few weeks later I started arguing with Officer Vermaak again. I had two homemade shanks (knives) and chased him down the prison corridor. Before I reached him I was wrestled to the ground and after receiving the standard beating was sent to Brandvlei prison which at the time was one of the most notorious prisons in South Africa and still is.

I have seen men here with their heads almost severed from their bodies. I was in medium cell block Z, and needed to get to maximum security because the number had no power in medium. I hit a prisoner with a brick and was sent to maximum security.

I was now in maximum with some of my Home Boys and I loved it here. I needed to get my sergeant stripes. I saw a 26 walk past our cell and hit him with a brick then I pulled him into the cell and raped him before stabbing him several times in front of the other 28s. He was a virgin and I loved it. I got my sergeant stripes and life in prison just was another part of my lifestyle.

I was released in 1995 and returned to Mitchell's Plain where I once again met up with my friend Azad. We started to pimp women. I pimped out my daughter's mother and around this time we also started to sell ecstasy in the clubs in Cape Town. We would also wrap Grandpa Headache powder and sell it as cocaine to unsuspecting tourists in Long Street, Cape Town.

I then met a Zulu girl called Princess. I started dating her and after spending a weekend with me she went home to her parents in Khayelitsha I didn't see her until two weeks later on the train sitting with her aunt and uncle. I was with Azad and Mongrel and Pretty boy.

I asked her where she had been and she pretended not to know me. When the train stopped at the next station we threw her aunt and uncle off the train. We were drinking and smoking mandrax and I told Princess to keep quiet or I would stab her.

When we got to Cape Town central Azad said he was going to collect money from his girlfriend who was selling herself at one of the local seaman's clubs. Mongrel and I got picked up by some other Home Boys and took Princess to a derelict building where I had sex with her. I then told Mongrel to have sex with her as well. We got back in the car and were waiting for Azad.

Princess was in the back seat between Mongrel and me. A police van pulled up and asked what we were doing, whereupon Princess started screaming for help and that she had been raped. They pulled Mongrel and I from the car, handcuffed us and made us sit on the pavement.

Azad arrived and the police wanted to arrest him but Princess told the police that he had nothing to do with the abduction and rape. We were both arrested and charged with kidnapping and rape. Both Mongrel and I got ten years for our crime. The two other HLs got suspended sentences. I was back in Pollsmoor and met Imran, who also happened to be Azad's big brother.

Imran AKA the enforcer

I was living in Mannenberg on the Cape Flats and at the age of six joined a gang called The Zaraks. My cousin Hare (Hair) was the leader of the gang he was sixteen years old. I was taught how to shoplift and any money we got was used to buy glue and petrol for sniffing.

When I was eight, I stole a bus conductor's money pouch in Wynberg. I got a train back to Mannenberg and went to an empty piece of land known as Die Boss (The Bush). I had bought a bottle of petrol, a packet of ten Gold Dollar cigarettes and a box of matches.

I was on my own and was sniffing the petrol. I put the petrol on my lap and then lit a cigarette, I threw the match to the ground but it hit the bottle on the way down, it caught alight and I jumped up, spilling the burning petrol all over myself. I was screaming and in severe pain and some people nearby came running over and managed after what seemed like forever to put the flames out. I was in agony and was blacking in and out of consciousness as the ambulance took me to Groote Schuur hospital where I spent the next year recuperating.

When I was discharged from hospital I returned to my old ways of stealing and sometimes would deliver drugs. I wasn't long before I was sent to Bonnytown reformatory, not long after that I was sent to Swartklip reformatory in Pretoria.

The boys here ranged from toddlers to sixteen years old. The food was good but we did not do any sport activities and when not in school used to just hang around the dormitories. There were many gangs here: Scorpions, Born Frees and Kaffir Slagters. I was a Scorpion and often had fights with Kaffir Slagters as they were also the outsiders, most being from Johannesburg and Pretoria.

These were not our Home Boys. There were mostly coloured and blacks as it was still segregated during apartheid.

We would work at the local golf course as caddies and could earn as much as R20 a day. We'd go on outings with the reformatory but had to pay for it ourselves, it cost 75 cents per outing. I was growing up fast and we were constantly fighting rivals. Now it was not only just fists but knives and bricks. When a Scorpion got badly hurt he had to stab a rival gang member when he got better. Many boys ended up in hospital after gang fights.

I was now 15 and spent holidays with my dad who lived in District Six which is best known for the forced removal of 60 000 inhabitants during the late1960s to 1980s by the apartheid regime.

After World War II, during the earlier part of apartheid, District Six was relatively cosmopolitan. Situated within sight of the harbour, it was made up largely of coloured residents which included a substantial number of coloured Muslims, called Cape Malays There were also a number of black Xhosa residents and a small numbers of whites, and Indians.

Government officials gave four primary reasons for the removals. In accordance with apartheid philosophy, it stated that interracial interaction bred conflict, necessitating the separation of the races. They deemed District Six a slum, fit only for clearance, not rehabilitation. They also portrayed the area as crime-ridden and dangerous; they claimed that the district was a vice den, full of immoral activities like gambling, drinking, and prostitution. Though these were the official reasons, most residents believed that the government sought the land because of its proximity to the city centre, Table Mountain and the harbour.

On 11 February 1966, the government declared District Six a whites-only area, with removals starting in 1968. By 1982, more than 60 000 people had been relocated to the sandy, bleak Cape Flats 25 kilometres away. The houses were bulldozed. The only buildings left standing were places of worship. However, local and International pressure made redevelopment difficult for the government. The Cape Technikon (now Cape Peninsula University of Technology) was built on a portion of District Six which the government renamed Zonnebloem.

By 2003, rebuilding had started on the first new buildings: 24 houses which will belong to residents over 80 years old. On 11 February 2004, former president Nelson Mandela handed the keys to the first returning residents, Ebrahim Murat (87) and Dan Ndzabela (82). About 1 600 families were scheduled to return over the next few years).

The gangs operating here were The Jesters, Bun Boys. The BOK's, and of course, the Scorpions. There was lots of fighting here over who owned the territory for dealing of drugs.

I heard that my sister and brother had been missing from home

41

for a week and went looking for them. My mother, who lived in Mannenberg, was beside herself in the moments when she was sober or in between drug binges.

I found them at a friend of the family and they told me that my mother's new husband was beating them. I got some Scorpions together and went to the house and told the child beater to come outside. He was drunk and stoned, he laughed at me and asked what a pipsqueak like me could do. He was a big man and as he lunged for me I stepped aside and hit him with a baseball bat over his head and then all the other boys piled into him punching and kicking him until he was unconscious. The next day he packed his bags and we never heard from him again.

I just turned sixteen when Lemme (blades) and I went shoplifting. Lemme was older and had been in and out of prison most of his adult life.

We went to The Golden Acre in Cape Town looking for a place that sold perfume. A security guard had been following us around as he was suspicious of us but couldn't prove theft. We decided to leave but Lemme insisted we stay and get his new younger girlfriend Shenay some perfume.

He acted as a decoy and pretended to be looking at goods and then putting them down. I slipped a bottle of Chanel no 5 in my shopping back as this was the brand that Shenay used. We both left by the front exit simultaneously, where two security guards arrested us. We were both charged with theft, all they found on us was the bottle of Chanel no 5.

I told the Magistrate that I had stolen the bottle of perfume which was now state evidence. The Magistrate said that he did not believe me and that juveniles often took the blame so that the real perpetrator got away scot free.

He sent Lemme to jail for 15 years, saying that he was a repeat offender and perhaps he would learn his lesson this time. The magistrate set me free. Even to this day I find the justice system in

South Africa hard to understand, 15 years for a bottle of perfume and a crime that Lemme did not commit! There are many people who can tell you the same stories, sex offenders and murderers get less jail time than a hungry person stealing food.

It wasn't many years later that I got sent to Pollsmoor for seven years for a range of crimes, from armed robbery to shoplifting. Going into an adult prison is a very frightening experience because now I was a small fish in a big pond.

On arrival at prison I was ordered to strip naked and to squat, this is for two reasons. The first is to see by your tattoos which gang you are affiliated to and ranking. The second is to see if you are carrying any contraband in your anus. You are then assigned to a cell.

I received a severe beating on my first night but did not get raped. Another prisoner who arrived with me was.

I was watched by 'Die Glas' (The binoculars) who watches you to see what kind of person you are and how you treat others. I was a Frans and was put in a cell with the 26s. I was beaten and fought back if anyone tried to rape me. I was not going to become a woman in prison. I had to wash other prisoner's clothes and my food was taken from me.

After eighteen months the beatings got less and then I got to go on work parties at local farms. On Saturdays I worked on a farm for a farmer called Pieter Vlok. There were pigs, sheep and chickens, there were twenty-four of us. I got to work with the chickens cleaning their cages, because I was a Muslim. The farmer trusted us and would often leave us alone on the farm. I saw the opportunity and decided to rob the farmer.

One Saturday morning at ten am the farmer left us alone and drove away, I saw this as my opportunity and broke into the farmhouse. I was looking for something of value that I could easily hide and searched the house room by room.

In the master bedroom I found a box of jewels hidden in a draw under some clothing. I took rings and diamonds and swallowed as much as I could. We were sent back to prison for lunch at twelve midday. I ate a meal of corn on the cob. Then we were sent to our rooms until two pm for a resting period. I said nothing to anyone. After two pm it was a time to wash our two sets of clothes for Sunday inspection.

Before our resting period was over Pieter Vlok arrived at the prison brandishing a gun, all twenty-four workers were called to the office and Pieter approached me and screamed at me, saying he knew that I was the thief. Pieter said that all the other workers were too far from the main house and it could only have been me. We were all searched and had rectal examinations.

The farmer was screaming that the jewels were worth R250 000. I was shocked and knew that if any other prisoner found out it would be cut from my stomach, I was only a Frans and could not trust anyone.

We were all retuned to our cells and when I arrived in mine the 26s wanted to know where the jewels were. I said that I hadn't stolen the jewels but I was a known thief on the outside and they didn't believe me. I was beaten with a block of soap in a sock but still did not say anything. The first time I passed the jewels I washed them and did not know where to hide them so I swallowed them again and did so for the next two months.

One morning I was told that I was been transferred to Drakenstein Correctional Centre (formerly Victor Verster Prison) The prison is famous for being the prison where Nelson Mandela spent the last three of the 27 years he spent in prison for campaigning against Apartheid.

The 26s gave me five dagga stops(marijuana wrapped in newspaper) measuring five and a half inches long each and was told them to get them to the other 26s in Drakenstein. I had endured almost two years of abuse by the 26s and was having no more.

I approached the 28s and gave them the Dagga and asked for

protection, also asking to join their number. The numbers control every prison in South Africa and prior to mobile phones had a secretive system of communicating with other prisons, if you betray a gang you are not safe anywhere. Upon arrival at Drakenstein, the 26s asked where the Dagga was. I told them I did not know what they were talking about as I was a 28!

I still had the jewels inside me when arriving at Drakenstein and now knew it was the right time to dispose of them. I met a prisoner, Joey, whose mother was a jeweller who would buy stolen goods from time to time. I arranged to meet his mother on my next visit.

I met Joey's mother and she introduced herself as Mrs Cassim. I gave her a ring to look at and told her what else I had. She offered me R10 000 which I accepted and it was paid into my property at the prison before I handed over the balance of the jewels. Because I was an A category prisoner and I could meet my visitors face to face , other prisoners had glass separating them from visitors.

Prisoners get money paid into their property which is like an account but withdrawals can only be made once a week and the amount and goods you could purchase depended on the category prisoner you are.

The A category could withdraw R400 and buy sweets, sugar, tobacco, coffee, polish and soap. The B category could withdraw R250 a week and could only buy tobacco, soap, polish, coffee and sugar. The C category could withdraw R150 a week and could buy tobacco, soap, polish, coffee and sugar. The D category could withdraw R80 a week and could buy tobacco, soap, polish, coffee and sugar.

I was in favour with the 28s and now was recruited to join them. I was put in front of the council of four and asked 'why did you come here' and I said 'I want to fight for the law'. I answered correctly and was given a knife and told to stab a Frans.

I was stopped before the stabbing as this was the first test. Now I was accepted into the gang. Then I met with the council of four again and was instructed to stab a prison officer. I stabbed a prison officer in the arm. I was beaten nearly to death and then went back to court and got a further five years added to my sentence.

I was then taught the way of a soldier and was schooled into the 28s. I learnt that Friday is a day of rations. All possessions are collected in the cell and distributed according to rank. Saturday is the day of justice; this is when the judicial structure of the gang meets to pass sentence on an offender. Sunday is the day of rights, victories are celebrated, members are promoted and newcomers recruited into the family. In 1994 I was released with many other prisoners on amnesty by FW De Klerk

I continued my crime spree and then started housebreaking. We were still using women as spotters going to work as maids and checking the houses for us. These days it's easier, as we send them in with mobile phones and they picture everything for us, in this way we can steal on order.

Often I would steal jewellery and give it to my sisters but every time I got arrested the police would confiscate it from them. I had many good years of housebreaking but never got caught until a drug addict Rita got caught with a substantial amount of drugs and was going to prison for a long time. She made a deal with police and told them of our scheme. My fingerprints were found in many of the houses I robbed. I was arrested and sentenced to twenty years at Pollsmoor prison.

While in prison I was given an order by the number to kill another inmate. With the help of two others we stabbed the inmate to death. I was sentenced to a further nine years. I spent fifteen years in prison. I got released in April 2012 and had to go and live with my family of Hard Livings.

These are the only people I know and do not have any other future.

Prison does not reform you; it only makes you more of a criminal.

I am going straight and not committing any more crime and will avoid prison at all cost.

As I walked away I noticed Imran selling some drugs to a punter that had just arrived at The Complex. As I got in my car and drove away a song came on the radio. It was *Gangster's paradise* ...

Amaal

If Only

I come from a very large family. We were nine children, all brought up in the Muslim faith although my one sister converted to Christianity.

I was the eldest daughter and it was expected of me from a young age to assist with my other siblings. Our house was not very big and sometimes my mother used to sleep outside, this was often in a drugged drunken stupor. Some days there was no food or electricity. My mother ran a shebeen (selling alcohol illegally) and sold drugs from home. The area was rife with gangsters. I was seven years old when my sister, two brothers and I were sent to go live with my granny in Hanover Park on the Cape Flats.

We shared this house with my granny, two of my uncles, their wives and three of their children. There wasn't much space so the only place where we could sleep was in the bathroom, which was not only cramped, but we would also have to take turns to sleep in the bath. We had no pillows and only two very thin sheets to cover us. We were often woken several times during the night when one of the twelve occupants of the house needed the toilet. My aunts and uncles often put their feet on us when they were sitting on the toilet.

There were often arguments with our cousins who were not much older than us but no matter if they were right or wrong, we always got beaten. Our cousins got to watch television but we were always sent to our makeshift bed in the bathroom early. Gifts were always bought on birthdays only for our cousins and we were reminded how grateful we ought to be. We were woken very early in the mornings to start with the household chores, during which time our cousins were sleeping in their warm soft cozy beds.

One morning after we'd finished our household chores my granny called me and my sister to her room and told us that we were going to a party the next day if we were good. Our brothers did not seem bothered that they were not going. We could hardly contain our excitement that night and the next morning got up extra early to complete our chores. We got dressed and my aunt put a new ribbon in each of our hair. We felt like princesses that morning as this would be the first party we would ever attend.

Our uncle drove us at ten that morning in his brand new car. At this point, in our excitement, we still did not ask whose party we were going to. We drove and we were giggling so much that our uncle told us to be quiet or we'd be going home. We sat in silence but could hardly contain our excitement.

We arrived at a big old brick building that looked like an old school. Our uncle took some bags out of the boot of the car but we were too excited to notice. An elderly woman dressed up in white with a beautiful kind face opened the door and welcomed us in. I asked where the balloons, streamers and cakes were for the big party?

My uncle told us not to be stupid as this was our new home and this is where we were to stay from now on. We burst into tears not because we were sorry to leave the only home that we knew, but because of the betrayal of my granny, uncles and aunts. This was our first day at St George's Catholic Orphanage, I was eight years old.

The orphanage turned out to be a blessing as we now had our own beds, slept warmly at night and had full bellies, we even got pocket money. Soon things turned out even better because we were taught how to swim, ride a bike and were also given toys.

I'll never forget our first Christmas in the orphanage, never had I seen so much food, cakes, a Christmas tree and there were presents! I remember opening my present and my heart skipped a beat as I saw the most beautiful doll ever, it was Princess Barbie. From that day I felt like a princess and all the bad was a distant memory.

We started getting weekend visits to see my mother. I had now been in the orphanage for two years and still was extremely happy. One weekend, a few days after my tenth birthday, I was at my mother's in Mannenberg. She had been drinking all day with some male friends and chased the kids outside to go and play. When it started getting dark I asked her if I could get something to eat and go inside, she swore at me and told me it was still early.

I decided to go for a walk by myself. I was crossing a field when two boys approached me and asked me where I was going and I said nowhere. They asked if I wanted to play a game and I said yes. They said that the game involved me taking all my clothes off. I started to get very frightened and knew that something bad was going to happen.

They pushed me to the ground and pulled my panties off. The next thing I felt was the worst pain ever. I was crying and begging them to stop but they would not. I do not know how long it carried on for but I just went numb and much later the boys just left. I was left crying in a heap. I cleaned the blood between my legs with an old cloth I found on my way home. I felt ashamed and dirty. I'd heard of bad girls who did such things but couldn't understand why they'd put themselves through so much pain.

It was very dark when I got home. Before I could say anything to my mother she shouted at me and asked where I had been so late and told me to go straight to bed. I still tied to explain but she gave me a smack across the face and told me to get to bed immediately. I was only 10 years old. This was the first time I was raped and I never felt so alone, I was too ashamed to even tell my sister.

Over the next two years I avoided going home as much as I could and when I got home my mother would make me clean and feed anyone who was in the house. My brothers were also in an orphanage and would also go to mother's for weekends. They had already joined the Hard Livings gang and often the gangsters would hang around our house. Mother did not care much as my brothers would give her money, alcohol and drugs. One day my sister and I were summoned to the mother superior's office at the orphanage. She told us that were going home to stay with our mother, we begged her in tears but she said that it was out of her hands. This was the beginning of the nightmare that I call my life.

Life at home was as bad as ever, I had to do household chores every day before school and often on my return the house would be in a mess and full of my brother's friends. There was smoking of Mandrax, drinking and loud music blaring till the early hours of the morning.

Several months later I met two boys in an area known as Bo-Kaap. One was called Scarface as he had a scar from cheek to cheek that he got in a gang fight; the other was called Ogies (eyes) as he had extremely green eyes for a coloured man. We became great friends and although they were both only 14, they were street wise.

Soon they were showing me how to pickpocket people in central Cape Town. They'd do most of the stealing and I would have a small bag of shopping where we would hide the wallets, watches or anything else they had stolen. We would keep the cash and sell anything else to a local dealer who gave us a 10th of what the goods were worth but we were quite happy just to get rid of it. With the money we would buy wine and cigarettes and would sit in empty houses or building sites and get drunk.

I was having a very hard time at school and found it very hard to concentrate, often hardly getting any sleep some nights. We had a school function one Friday night and it finished at about nine. My brother was to meet me at the school but never turned up. I decided to walk home but knew that there were lots of gangsters on the way home.

While passing an alley I was pulled in and shoved to the ground by three boys. They started strangling me and told me if I screamed they would kill me. Two of the boys raped me while the third one masturbated. They hurt me very badly. I was bleeding and had torn clothes. I was afraid to go home and ran to where I knew my dad lived. I didn't see him often because he also drank and smoked dagga and was incoherent most of the time.

When I arrived at his house he had friends there, they were drinking and smoking Mandrax. I was crying and told him what had happened. His response was: 'Well it is because you mix with bad people now go home!' I realised that I had no one I could turn to and I'd never felt so alone.

I arrived home much later and tried to sneak in through the back window. My bother Raj saw me and asked what had happened. I told him. He gave me a hug (very unusual, as a gangster he would never show affection) and said not to worry he would take care of it. He told my sister to take care of me.

I had told him what the boys looked like. They were from a rival gang, the Americans. I'm not sure what happened to the boys but they were not seen in the area again and nothing was said about it again. There had always been a dispute between the Americans and The Hard Livings. This was just another catalyst. That same year I left school.

The parties never stopped at home. Drugs and alcohol were used by almost everyone. I also started smoking dagga and drinking heavily.

In gang culture women do not join, but if you hang around gangsters they just take whomever they please, you have no choice.

I was taken by Lee when I was 14, he was 23. He forced himself on me and eventually I just submitted, thereafter he was kind to me and became my protector and taught me many things.

I recall when members of The Americans Gang were harassing me constantly on the train going to town daily. Lee got some members of the Hard Livings and waited for them on the train one day. Lee suddenly stabbed one of the boys in the neck. There was blood everywhere, everyone got such a fright that some people even jumped out of the moving train.

The next minute was chaotic as the rival gangs took each other on. There was so much blood it made me ill and I was relieved when the train stopped at the next station and I got off. Soon the police had arrived as the train driver had radioed ahead and many were arrested.

It was around this time that I fell pregnant. Once a fortnight I'd go to the clinic for a checkup. Getting to the clinic was not easy as I didn't have money for transport and often had to walk and without having eaten. I left home at eight in the morning and would only arrive at the clinic between 11 and 12.

My mother sometimes accompanied me but would swear and shout at me in front of everyone, saying: 'You are a slut you fucking scumbag, I was raped and you are the result and now you shame me more.' There was a very kind nurse who had beautiful blonde hair. Her name was Michelle, she often gave me food and spoke kindly to me, she also told my mother not to accompany me anymore.

Things were not getting better at home. The parties, drugs and abuse continued. I was at the lowest point of my life. My body was going through changes and I was in a deep state of depression. There was no one I could talk to and it would be another week before I could speak to my kind Michelle again.

I decided that I wanted to end my life and started planning the easiest way to do it. I knew where Lee had hidden all his drugs but I could not find it this time as he had been out dealing. I found some rat poison and was sitting on the edge of my bed. Suddenly I dropped to my knees and prayed to Allah.

A miracle happened, as there was a knock on my door and it was my brother Ashley. He came in and asked if I was okay and needed anything whereupon I burst into tears. He spoke to me very kindly and said that things always change and all we could do was hope. Ashley was a gangster and compassion and kindness was not one of his usual traits. I felt better and was grateful for his intervention. Fortunately he did not see the poison in my hand and to this day I have told no one about this.

My baby was born and I named her Anaum which means the blessing of Allah in Arabic. Things over the next three months went a bit smoother until one night my mother had taken a lot of drugs and threw me and Anaum out in the pouring rain.

By chance a local social worker happened to drive by and took me to my Aunt's house. I moved from there to my sister's house in Mitchell's Plain I had managed to get a job at a clothing factory as a machine operator .One night Anaum was breastfeeding and bit my nipple. It bled profusely and I was in a lot of pain. I couldn't get to work the next day and did not have money for a doctor.

I went to work the following day and the boss, Mr Hoffman, called me to his office. He told me I was fired before I could explain. He said that he also heard that I mixed with gangsters. He said that I had to get my things and leave immediately.

I dropped to my knees and begged him to please not do this, as it was all the money me and my baby had. He grinned at me and said it was not his problem and he was sick of people like me. I felt the anger in the pit my stomach and said to him to remember my face.

It was about a month later and at The Spring Queen Beauty pageant which was hosted for female employees who worked in the local factories. I arrived at the after party and spotted Mr

Hoffman. I walked up to him and said 'Do you remember me'? to which he replied 'Why should I'? Once again rage overtook me.

I jumped on him and he fell to the ground. I shouted 'I was the one you fired on my daughter's first birthday'. I started to strangle him, his face turned red, then blue. It took four big men to pull me off him. He was absolutely terrified and had urinated in his pants. As I was escorted off the premises I felt a smile creep onto my face and promised that from that day on no man would abuse me again ...... or so I thought.

I was lying in my room one night while Lee was out with his friends. There was a big party going on in another part of the house. I had Anaum next to me and I was dozing off. Suddenly a friend of my brother's slipped into bed behind me. Smelling of alcohol he said he wanted me and it was his right. I told him that I was Lee's woman and that he had better leave. I kicked him between the legs and he crumbled to the floor in pain. 'You stupid fucking bitch I will kill you,' he shouted but he left because Lee was not only a senior member of the gang, but was feared. This was a lucky escape and I knew I had to find a new place for me and the baby.

Gangsters would often use their women in any way they saw fit. Sometimes they were made to deal drugs and at other times we were made to sell our bodies.

The first time was terrible and I was terrified. Lee pimped me to an old man he knew, I do not even know how much he charged as I saw none of the money. I had smoked Mandrax. His name was Lex. He was overweight, short, balding, and smelt of body odour and alcohol. I just lay there and let him do what he had to. When he left I just crumbled into a fetal position and cried.

I then was sent to work in clubs in Cape Town, often frequented by sailors. Sometimes we would just get them drunk and rob them. If I liked someone I would book into a local hotel and spend the night. Lee was always close at hand and would take most of my money. Soon my sister's boyfriend Trevor was prostituting her as well. If the clubs were quiet we would go to an area known as Green Point and solicit our self on the street.

I would often just rob the punters of their money, knowing they would not go to the police and complain. We met Lucy in one of the clubs and she told me that she had a client that paid a lot of money and that she would introduce me to a friend of his.

A few days later Lucy took me to a private club. It smelt musky and the lighting was very dim so I could not see clearly. Lucy started whispering in Chinese to a man and I could not understand what she was saying. She introduced him as Mr Wong and left. He told me to relax and offered me a drink of Whisky and soda which I gulped down in one sip. I started feeling woozy and blacked out.

When I awoke I could just barely see as I was still disorientated. Then I saw a bright light and the outline of several naked men standing next to me there was also another man having sex with me. I could not move or speak but was fully aware of what was happening.

The men took turns raping and sodomising me while filming the whole event. I blacked out several times and woke up in an alley bleeding profusely, partially clothed and with a splitting headache. It was getting light and I managed to crawl to the pavement and called for help.

A man was walking past and I asked if he could please help me. He lowered his head and mumbled he was busy, and then hurried off. I must have lay there for at least an hour before one of the street cleaners coming on duty helped me. I was taken to hospital and treated for severe tears in my vagina and anus. It was several weeks before I could even walk properly again. I swore that I would get revenge. Lucy had disappeared and rumour on the street was that she was had left for Hong Kong.

I could not work as a call girl and although Lee was angry with me, he did not force me to go back to work the streets. I managed to get a job working in a Chinese restaurant called The Golden Lion in Sea Point. I worked in the kitchen. I had to work with pork and could not stand the smell but needed the money and as a Muslim it was forbidden … but I had bigger things on my mind. Several weeks later I got my sister a job as a waitress. Once the customers were served, I would leave the kitchen and speak to her in the serving area where you could view the customers without them seeing you.

We had been working there for three months quite happily when one night everything changed. I was in the serving area talking to my sister when I felt my blood run cold. Sitting in the restaurant I spotted not only Mr Wong but also two of my perpetrators. The only person I had told was my sister and when she saw how pale I was, and where I was staring, she knew.

My sister was the first to talk as a million different things were running through my brain. She asked what we should do. I composed myself and knew that calling the police was not an option. This was my opportunity for revenge and I was not going to let this opportunity pass me by. But before we said another word all hell broke loose. Armed men burst into the restaurant demanding that everyone lie on the floor. If this was my last day alive, who would look after my daughter was the only thought I had.

The next words I heard were 'Police, everybody stay calm and do not move'. I felt a sense of relief, not quite knowing what was going on. The table they had their attention on was none other than Mr Wong and his entourage. They were all handcuffed and taken away in several police vehicles.

It was only the next day that everything became clear. Mr Wong was a Mr Big in the Cape Town drug trade and was in the process of selling 5kg of cocaine, and was caught with the drugs in a briefcase handcuffed to his arm. For this and other related crimes Mr Wong got fifteen years in prison and two of the men who raped me – now known as Lok and Ming – got ten years each. All were sent to Pollsmoor prison. My brother was serving a ten-year sentence there and had been in and out of prison for many years. He is a 28 and a general. Now I knew justice would be served.

On my next visit to pollsmoor I told my brother everything that had happened to me and who was responsible. I heard later that all three men were first gang-raped and beaten and then given a 'slow puncture' or 'slow death' (where the anus is cut open and then one is raped by an HIV-positive inmate). I never heard anything about this again and put it all behind me.

I could not bear to stay at The Golden Lion any more as whenever I looked at the table I could still see Mr Wong and his cronies. The smell of pork in the kitchen was also a deciding factor to leave. I left Sea Point and moved to Manenberg.

Soon after I got a job in a factory that made chilli sauces for a company called Hot Foods in Salt River. My sister joined me once again. Unfortunately travel costs got to high and we had to leave. We started a shebeen (selling alcohol illegally from home) with my mother who was an expert in such things. We soon progressed to selling drugs.

Lee was no longer on the scene and now I was smoking a lot of Mandrax and also started using 'tik" (Chrystal meth). I decided to go back to selling my body for my new found addiction. I was still young, only 19 and pretty and used to frequent the clubs and pubs where middle age men hung out. I got many customers this way and all were white and very nice to me. I used to make from R150 to R2 500 (R10 = $1 USD or R17 = 1 GBP) per customer depending on how desperate I was for my next fix. Men used to take me to their hotels or homes and later, when I had enough money, I once again got an apartment in Sea Point and often would take punters there.

I met a very nice businessman from Johannesburg called Dwayne. Dwayne was a very kind man and did not want me to sleep

59

with other men and started giving me an allowance and paying all my bills. He was nursing a sick wife Jill, who had motor neuron disease and promised to stay with his wife until she died. He also told her about us and she gave us her blessing. I felt emotions for Dwayne that I never felt for any man before. He was patient, kind, knew everything about me and did not judge me, was this love I was feeling for the first time?

Dwayne was more than a client and over the next four years he made me feel like a princess again. We would go on holidays up the coast and he would buy Anaum and me many presents. On my 23rd birthday Dwayne bought me the most beautiful pearl necklace. It was the most expensive thing I ever owned.

It was a few days after my birthday that Dwayne's wife died. Dwayne went into a deep depression. I was at my wits end and did not know what to do. Dwayne never took any drugs but would occasionally smoke a joint. He was now spending more time with me and was neglecting his business in Johannesburg. One evening he asked me to please give him something stronger. I had not touched any 'tik' for several years and that evening Dwayne and I smoked our first pipe together This was to be one of the biggest regrets of my life because a few weeks later Dwayne was smoking 'tik' every day. His business took strain and he left his partner Mario in charge.

He got a call one Monday morning after being awake for three days from his lawyers saying that not only was his business bankrupt, but his private assets were not protected and he was losing everything.

This just pushed Dwayne over the edge and he was smoking twice as much and using any drugs he could get his hands on. A few weeks later after Dwayne had been awake for two days he walked into the kitchen saying he felt unwell. He clutched his chest and dropped dead on the floor of a heart attack. My fairytale once again had turned into a nightmare.

I went through the next few years in a daze, once again selling my body to not only feed my child but to also to supply my habit. I moved to a house in Green Point where there were about 10 working girls and most had their own pimps. I was in charge of taking money from the Punters. I was known to be connected to 'The Hard Livings' and soon a member, Pete, took me as his woman and also became my pimp.

The house got raided and I moved to another house across the road. I had a flat at the back of the house with my own private entrance, often I used to let gay friends of mine stay with me, many of them were also on the game and were rent boys.

I was in the flat one evening with my gay friend Rudie when two men burst into the flat and started yelling 'Where are the pills and the money? Where are the pills and the money?' I told them that there were no pills or money which was not true, as I had most of the girl's drugs and also kept their money.

They then pistol whipped Rudie, smashing his nose and kicking him as he fell to the ground. The one man who spoke said they could kill both of us and no one would know because they were the police and could do as they pleased.

One of them also said to me 'We know where Anaum is now and if you do not give us the drugs we will first kill you then her'. I went to my hiding place and took the drugs and money and handed it over. They left without another word. I do not know if they were police or not because they were wearing plain clothes but policeman were known visit the brothel and these men just seemed to know too much.

The pimps in the house were mad at me and demanded I pay back everything taken from me. I could not and did not know what to do, knowing that some wanted retaliation and I was their only target.

My sister had been dating a man called Barry who was a well known 'American'. He also started pimping her at the house at the time, her money was taken with all the other girl's money and drugs. A few days later she said to me 'I need to tell you something this evening. I will see you later'.

That evening I was on the couch watching a DVD with Pete and Anaum when I had a strange feeling, a feeling of impending doom. There was a knock on the door. We had put in a security gate. I told Pete to not open the gate but he was in the kitchen next to the door and didn't heard me.

As he opened the door six men stormed in and started beating Pete and me with steel pipes. I shouted to Anaum to run to the bedroom but she just froze. The men tied us all up and tied Anaum's one arm to mine. They then ripped off all my clothes and did the same to Pete. They proceeded to rape me and sodomize Pete. I was begging them not to harm my baby as she was only eight years old. I prayed out loud to Allah and said rather kill me than let them hurt my child. By some miracle they left her alone and left.

After some time I told Anaum to untie us as she still had one hand free, she did so in utter silence. I only had a head scarf and put it around my body, I felt so ashamed that my daughter had to witness this terrible event. When she saw me doing this she broke down and started crying hysterically. I knew that it would scar her for life. We called the police and gave statements.

I recognised two of the men as I had seen them in the house before. I gave police descriptions of the men I recognised. We heard later that evening the same six men went to another brothel, shot and killed two men and were all arrested. The problem was that these men were thought to be from the 'Americans' and I knew that we were going to need more protection than what was on offer.

The police took Anaum, Pete and I to a hotel for a few days first. This went on for a month and we weren't aware of what was going on. Soon after that the police put Anaum and I on a bus to Durban where they gave us accommodation in a three bed roomed house a few kilometres out of town; they also gave us money for food.

We were now in a place where we knew no one; I felt Isolated and decided to contact a former punter, Willem, who lived in Durban. He checked us in at the Umhlanga Sands Hotel and was very kind at first.

I knew Willem was married and that he and his wife were both racist. He said that after the kids were born she no longer gave him sex. He slept with only coloured prostitutes because it was his way of punishing her.

Willem was demanding sex continuously and got angry if I did not submit, I was recuperating from a trauma and rape and he could not care less. It was time to leave again and Anaum and I took a train back to Cape Town where we moved in with friends of the family in an area known as Brooklyn.

Several months later I had to go to the Magistrate's court in Cape Town to testify against the men who had attacked Pete and me. I had lost touch with Pete and was looking forward to seeing him again. Before the court proceedings started the prosecutors in the case asked to address the court.

I felt the blood drain from my face as the prosecutor informed the court that Pete had taken a fatal drug overdose. He left a note in which he had said that he could not stand the shame and humiliation of repeating the events of that terrible evening. The case was postponed and after six months was thrown out of court for missing documentation. It is common knowledge that if you found a corrupt policeman, any case can be won for the right money.

Anaum was growing up and when I saw what was happening to her, it was history repeating itself. There was only one person to blame and that was myself.

We had once again moved to Woodstock and Anaum had made some good friends at first and I was pleased as she seemed so much happier. She had just turned 13 when I noticed a change in her.

I gave her money for food and often had to leave her alone

when I went back to selling drugs and my body. I look back and realise that what she needed was my love and time – and not money. To give material things means nothing, to give of yourself is everything.

We often had policemen that came and drank with us and took drugs. These were the ones whom we could also bribe and women, drink and drugs was one of the perks for them. One evening we were having a party and one of the police officers, (still in full uniform) with a joint in his hand and a glass of vodka in the other, asked if I knew where Anaum was.

I asked him what he meant as she was staying at a friend's house whose mother I knew well. He replied that that was not true, as he had seen her not long ago in Giempie Street which was notorious for drugs. I got a taxi to Giempie Street and knew that there were many gangsters that would ply young girls with drugs and drink and then use them.

I arrived a little after ten and could hear music blaring from several houses, on a corner I saw a group of teenagers drinking and there, standing with a cigarette in her mouth and a bottle of wine in the other, was Anaum. I just went berserk. I was screaming and pulling her by her hair and asking her if she knew what would happen if she continued with this lifestyle? Anaum just looked at me calmly and said 'Yes Mum, I will become just like you'.'

Anaum became more and more difficult. She was now fourteen and using ecstasy and mandrax. I had now been married to a man called Ismael who was a muslim, but also a gangster. He used to drink and now also started using drugs.

Anaum stole money from me all the time, one day she stole ten 'Rocks' from me, which were R120 (R17 = 1 British Pound or R11 = 1 United States Dollar) each. They would blame each other and I was caught in the middle. I got so stressed that I got shingles. Anaum now was staying out all night. Ismael used to be away for a week and when he returned, Anaum would stay away for a week. If Ismael stayed out two days, Anuam would stay out two days; it was like a power struggle between the two of them.

Anaum was now using tik and I felt so helpless that I even laid a charge of theft against her, hoping she would be arrested. I asked the police if we could send her to rehab and he said because she was a juvenile I could check her in. Anuam ran away and did not return for a month and on her return said if I tried to send her to rehab, I would never see her again.

A few months after her 17th birthday Anaum gave birth to a baby girl and named her Aisha. When I arrived at the hospital she held the baby to me in outstretched arms and said 'Mommy this is for you'. Fortunately Aisha had no withdrawal symptoms and I just gave her lots of vitamins. Two years later she gave birth to a boy Dejamo and a year later to another boy Hassam.

Anaum was now dating a 'Hard Livings' gangster who was a 'Gifted Kid' gang member first before joining the HLs. Magoodien was also a drug dealer and user, Anaum and Magoodien would use drugs in front of the children and she sometimes was so out of it that I had to look after the kids for days.

I was running a little tuck shop selling sweets, cool drinks and cigarettes. Anaum was stealing from me all the time. She knew where I kept all the valuables in the house and once broke into the safe where I used to hide gangsters money and drugs. To this day I still do not know how she'd done it. She pointed out to me on many occasions that I was no better than her. Although I did not want to admit this, somehow I knew it was true.

Anaum was admitted at Groote Schuur Hospital on the 14th March 2012 after being diagnosed with tuberculosis. She was kept there for seven days and was then transferred to Brooklyn Chest Hospital. She was then sent back to Groote Schuur.

I was approached by the South African Police Service on the 21st March 2012 (Human Rights Day) and told that my daughter

Anaum had passed away. I was informed by Detective Van Wyk of Woodstock SAPS when I entered Ward C15 at Groote Schuur that the woman in the bed next to Anaum had stabbed her in the chest. The hospital however stated that Anaum had committed suicide by falling on a broken plate and then later said that the plate had fallen on the floor and while picking the plate up she had fallen on it.

Amaal attempted numerous times to obtain information regarding her daughter's death, but it seemed that the Woodstock SAPS had taken Detective Van Wyk off the matter and a certain Detective Jones of Woodstock SAPS took over. No criminal case was ever opened and no death inquest was initiated. Detective Jones kept on telling Amaal he was awaiting statements from the Hospital to take the matter further. However towards the end of December 2012 Detective Jones gave Amaal a copy of the Pathology report which stated that Anaum died as a result of multiple stab wounds to her chest.

Amal said the likelihood of Anuam having committed suicide by falling on a broken plate was not only preposterous, but also improbable. Anaum had three stab wounds to her chest. It seems unlikely that Anaum had placed the broken shards upright on the floor then intentionally fallen on it or that the plate had slipped out of her hand and in her attempt to pick up the broken plate she fell onto it and that caused the fatal stab wounds. The hospital version also seems at odds with why the patient in the bed next to Anaum's had never called for help.

Amaal's attorney instituted legal proceedings against the SAPS under the notice in terms of section 3(2) of the institution of legal proceedings against certain organs of state act of 2002. I am suing the South African Police Service and Groote Schuur for the negligent death of my daughter.

Amaal said that Groote Schuur Hospital had had a legal duty to

protect her daughter Anaum. The omission of the hospital to provide
some form of security to protect patients had lead to the death of her
daughter. Amaal said 'It has been more than a year and I just want
the truth on how my daughter died and for those responsible to be
brought to justice.'

'If Only I had done things differently, If Only I had never used drugs,
If Only I had never sold my body, If Only I was a better mother, If
Only ……

Andrew

I Blame the Government

I had a good but disciplined childhood. However, I could never please my father, no matter what I did. He would criticise me for everything and would always say that I was stupid. My mother was no better and I often got hit with the sjambok, a whip made of animal hide – whether I had done something wrong or not. I went to school many days covered in blue, purple marks from hidings with the sjambok. At school I was an average student, but didn't always conform and often found myself in the Headmaster's office for six of the best with his choice of wooden cane.

I went to an Afrikaans school in Durban where the discipline was extreme. The Vice Principle, known as Gaffs, was hated by all. Two of my school friends were often taken into the office and given six of the best. Their parents were poor and they were never given school fees. On other occasions he would give them six of the best each because they did not have short enough hair.

There was a group of us who were his main target, he constantly told us that we were useless and would never amount to anything. If there was a rumour of trouble in school, we were called to the office and punished – whether we were right or wrong.

Eventually he managed to expel my friend Johnny for smoking in his school uniform. Johnny was mad and really wanted revenge. He started drinking heavily, but he came from a good family and they convinced him to do his National Service early. Johnny did and joined the Special Forces and his hatred was directed at the enemy of the government.

Twenty five years later after all the bad things he endured he still has a hate for Gaffs. He opened an Antiques store on the west coast of Durban. He was broken into on many occasions and had lots of goods stolen but the police just told him that chances are the thief would never be caught. Johnny decided to sleep in his shop and one evening low and behold he caught the thief red-handed. Johnny had a gun pointed at the thief and told him calmly 'Bring back all the stuff that you have stolen and we will leave things as it is', to which the thief replied 'I am a professional thief and cannot do that'. Johnny said to him 'Well I am a killer trained by the government' and shot him in head, killing him instantly. After a short trial the defence won on the basis that Johnny was a government trained killer.

My poor friends became rich friends, one becoming a wealthy entrepreneur and one become a world famous author. I was not that lucky.

After school I was conscripted for my two years National Service. I was in the Infantry and became a non-commissioned officer in a short while and eventually ending up as a sergeant. I trained two companies of a hundred men each and accompanied them on their tour of duty lasting three months each respectively.

After my national service I returned to Durban where I became a train driver. The hours were long but the money was so good that I could buy a brand new car and furnish my new apartment. I was only twenty years old and life was good. I met my girlfriend and it was not long before she moved in with me and a few years later we were married.

I was working late one night when my wife called me in tears saying that a particular policeman had been extremely rude and aggressive with her. When I returned home later that evening my wife was still very upset and she proceeded to tell me what had happened.

Susan told me that this was not the first time that she had encountered this policeman. He used to visit our neighbours, and had made an advance towards Susan on a previous occasion. When she told him that she was married and not interested he just laughed. On this occasion he told her that she could not park in front of the apartment block and had to move immediately even though there were no lines or signs prohibiting parking.

Andrew was angry and went next door to ask the neighbour where the policeman was. He just happened to be off duty in civilian clothing and sitting in the lounge. Andrew confronted the policeman and asked him why he was harassing his wife. The policeman told him that he was cop and could do as he pleased. This enraged Andrew even more, as here was this policeman, barely twenty years old, who'd probably joined the police to avoid conscription, being facetious. Andrew lost his temper and physically beat him until he cried for Andrew to stop. The policeman said he was sorry and that it would not happen again. Andrew apologised to his neighbour and left.

The next morning at about five, Andrew was getting ready for work when there was a knock on the door. Standing at the door were two policemen telling Andrew that he was being arrested for GBH (grievous bodily harm) He was taken to the local police station where he was charged and later bailed by his wife. The court case was set for three months later. Andrew and Susan were not worried about the case because Andrew had never committed a crime before and this was a first offence.

The court case arrived and in the witness box the policeman stated that it was Andrew who was harassing him. The magistrate sent Andrew to prison for nine months.

My first night in prison was strange but I wasn't afraid, having been to the military. I was also familiar with armed combat. However in prison I knew things worked differently and here I was a very small fish in a very big pond. I approached one of the prisoners in the cell and asked who was in charge of the cell.

I was directed to Gert, an Afrikaner who was serving life for killing his wife and the man she was having an affair with. I told Gert that my wife would pay money into my property and I would give him a third of what I got to ensure I had protection and would not be harassed by other prisoners. Gert agreed.

After my first week in prison I realised that there were quite a few men who did not have anyone on the outside to send them money. I saw this as an opportunity and soon had five men getting money paid into their property of which they kept a third. Now I could just about get anything I wanted in prison except female company, which meant my wife of course. In prison the value of money or anything else of value, be it cigarettes, sweets, alcohol, is tenfold.

These were apartheid years and we were segregated from prisoners of colour, not that we had any more privileges. In prison you become a criminologist and learn more about crime than some lawyers do.

I soon learned how to smuggle drugs into prison, my choice of drug was Mandrax smoked with marijuana. We used a pigeon that we fed to smuggle drugs into prison. We also had a cat that we used to strap our contraband to, we had someone on the outside to feed him and he used to be fed and slept with us. We called the cat Bandit, which was suitable because the cat did not like the prison officers either and would run away when approached by them. They shot and killed the cat one day because no pets were aloud and they had their suspicions.

There were some very bad times in prison when I was not goofed (a slang term used in Durban when someone is high after smoking marijuana). And even the drugs could not block out the badness happening around me.

One late afternoon a young boy Tim, who was only nineteen, got assigned to our cell after he was sentenced to twelve months for shoplifting, this was his first offence. One of the older inmates homed in on him and offered him a cigarette and then also gave him some sweets.

Tim thought that this was going to be easy prison time but what he did not realise was that he would have to pay back in one way or another. It was soon established that Tim was an orphan and had no one on the outside to support him and pay money into his property. That night we had to endure his screams as he was raped time and time again until later all we heard was his sobbing. In prison you do not interfere as this could cost you your life.

Not long after there was a dispute over R2.00 Drug debt in today's market that would be about R250.00 is multiplied by ten in prison. Piet was twenty nine years old and doing a ten-year sentence for armed robbery, he was waiting for money to be transferred onto his property when his girlfriend met someone else on the outside and thus no longer was paying into his property. He was in the shower one day when another prisoner came up behind him and cut his jugular vein with a razor blade. By the time the prison officers arrived he was lying dead in a pool of blood.

Susan still kept her sense of humour and on one occasion sent a request on a local radio station for a song for her husband in prison. When the song 'I want to break free' by Queen came on, both prison officials and prisoners had a good giggle. Susan went to visit Andrew in prison whenever there was a visit available and on every occasion he was totally high. Susan was not pleased but realised that this was a terrible place and Andrew was just trying to block out this nightmare. She thought that all would go back to normal once he was released, how wrong she was.

Andrew was released after only three months for good behaviour. He told his work on returning the truth about his incarceration and they told him if they had known, he would not have spent one day in

73

prison. Andrew got a transfer to Cape Town and soon after Susan and Andrew moved to Cape Town.

They first moved to an apartment in Sea Point and six months later bought a beautiful three-bedroom house in the suburb of Tableview. Nine months later their son Jared was born. Andrew was still smoking mandrax but hiding it from Susan as best he could.

Andrew had many friends but also had his drug-taking friends whom he was spending more time with. When his son Jared was born both parents were overjoyed. Susan was hoping that Andrew would now change his ways, which he initially did. Eighteen months later Kendra was born and life was looking good for the family.

Unfortunately life was not to be that kind when nine months later Kendra fell ill. Both Susan and Andrew were beside themselves when their paediatrician could not diagnose their daughter's illness saying that it was something that she had eaten and was allergic to. Susan, being a nursing sister, did her own investigating and discovered that whenever Kendra would eat anything she would vomit her food up whole. When she was a nurse she'd seen the same symptoms in children who had brain tumours.

Susan asked her paediatrician for a brain scan as she suspected that her daughter had a brain tumour, her paediatrician deemed it unnecessary. Susan asked her doctor if he could send her daughter for a brain scan and a brain tumour was found.

Kendra was taken into surgery the following morning and the tumour was removed. This was only the beginning of many months of chemotherapy. Andrew decided to resign from work and take a retirement package so that he could look after Kendra. He found it hard to see his daughter in so much pain and opted not to attend chemotherapy sessions at hospital with Susan, choosing rather to nurse her on her return home.

A few years later Jared was diagnosed with ADHD (Attention

Deficit Hyperactivity Disorder). Susan and Andrew thought that perhaps all the attention that was spent on Kendra had caused this. They decided not to medicate Jared but decided to sell their property in Tableview and buy a farm in Malmesbury. This was the right choice for the children but Andrew soon went back to his old habits.

He soon found some local drug dealers and continued smoking mandrax, but besides his habit continued to be an exceptional father. Susan was travelling to work every day, making a two-hour roundtrip from Cape Town to Malmesbury. Susan had also been studying accountancy and now was working for an accounting firm and studying by correspondence over a five-year period to qualify.

Andrew and Susan would on many occasions let friends and family who'd lost jobs and homes stay on the farm.

Andrews's mother, who lived in Durban, retired and wanted to spend time with her grandchildren. Andrew and Susan were both overjoyed when Katrina moved in with them. Andrew had always been very close to his mother after his parents divorced when he was still a toddler.

Katrina was very good with the children and this gave Andrew time to tend to his farm and livestock.

Katrina was still old school and believed that children should be seen and not heard. Often, if any of the kids made a mistake with a task, she's berate them, telling them they were stupid. This infuriated Susan because Kendra had some learning difficult as a result of her illness.

Susan told Katrina that if she ever disrespected her kids again that she would not be welcome in her home anymore, after this the matter was resolved.

Jared was very bright and the farm life had kept his busy mind occupied, he also attended the local school where he did not only excell academically, but on the sports field as well. Kendra was home-schooled.

Andrew was still unsettled in Malmesbury and decided to sell and look further afield for another farm; they found the perfect farm 5km outside Langebaan on the West coast. They also bought a house in Langebaan where they have lived for the past eighteen years. Katrina moved with them but would visit her other daughter in Durban from time to time. Katrina still had an apartment in Durban which she was now renting out.

Kendra was still home schooled and now had some other kids to join her. Although Andrew and Susan were brought up during the apartheid era there was no racism in their home and children and adults of all ethnic backgrounds were welcome in their house. Jared attended the local school and in no time had many friends.

Life carried on at home and things were running smoothly until one day when Andrew was coming down from a Mandrax binge. He shouted at Jared for not cleaning his room. Jared shrugged his shoulders in defiance and something deep inside Andrew snapped. Andrew lunged at Jared with a snarled up face shouting at the same time that he was going to get his first hiding ever.

Susan intervened and he turned his aggression towards her but before he got a foot from her, Katrina hit him with a sjambok several times. Andrew was stunned then shocked as he tried to fend off the painful blows. He decided that retreat was the best option. This was the first time since he was a teenager that his mother had beaten him. He was a grown man whose mother still commanded respect and she certainly got it.

On a few occasions Andrew would take drugs with a friend called Reggie. Reggie's choice of drug was tik which he bought from the local dealer and then smoked at Andrew's.

Andrew only ever smoked mandax and never kept any supplies at home, rather buying what he used on a daily basis. Reggie was forty years old and recently separated from his girlfriend. He was now staying with his mother.

One morning his mother was emptying his pockets before

doing the laundry whereupon she found a packet of tik. She went berserk and told Reggie to tell her where he had got the drugs or leave the house. Reggie could not give up the dealer because the repercussions would be far worse, even a hit on his life if the information got back to the dealer.

Reggie told his mother that Andrew had given him the drugs. Reggie's mother in turn contacted the local police and told them that not only was Andrew a drug dealer, but a manufacturer of tik. The police raided the house at four am one morning and searched the entire house, finding nothing.

On another occasion one of Jared's friends who had developed a drug habit was caught with a substantial amount of drugs. He was going to do a lot of prison time but made a plea bargain with the police, saying that Andrew was a drug dealer, smuggled Ivory, dealt in stolen vehicles and had obtained property illegally

The police arrived in eight vehicles at eight pm one evening, closing off the road in front of the house and brandishing automatic rifles and wearing full riot gear.

I was about to have a smoke when I heard the commotion outside, I hid my marijuana pipe in a nearby cupboard and the marijuana and mandrax pill under the cupboard. The police produced a warrant and searched the whole house; two policemen with a sniffer dog came into the place and started searching it. The police dog stopped in front of the cupboard and started barking; one of the policemen found the marijuana pipe and got very excited, calling his colleagues because now surely this was going to be the bust of the century! Unfortunately it was short-lived because they didn't find anything – not even the marijuana and pill under the cupboard.

The police asked me to accompany them as they searched the house, as we approached a room next to a door leading to an outside verandah; I warned the police that there was a staffie bull cross under the bed. The verandah door was open and as one of the policemen peered under the bed, my dog started barking.

The policemen got such a fright that he ran onto the verandah and jumped into the garden and into a pile of dog shit. I told the policeman that he was not getting back into the house until he washed his shoes, which he did.

I had a few marijuana plants right where the policeman jumped but he failed to see it. Before the police left Susan told them that not only had they wasted their resources, but that Andrew was an addict and only bought for his own use. She added that if they ever returned she would sue the police. They left and have not returned since.

Andrew never had a run in with the police but did with the gangsters and the dealers.

One evening my old 4x4 got stolen and then used in the robbery of a dealer. The vehicle was abandoned after the robbery in a nearby neighbourhood and I retrieved it the following day. I went to buy my local supply at the local dealer and when I stopped outside his house my car was surrounded by several gangsters. They recognised the car and thought that it was me who'd assisted in the robbery.

One of the gangsters pulled out a gun and another approached the driver's side with a machete. I told them that I had nothing to do with the robbery and that my vehicle had been stolen. One of the gangsters grabbed a hold of my shirt through the open window and in turn I grabbed hold of his arm and sped off dragging him with me. Once we were far enough away, I let him go.

There was now a hit out on me and I started using a different dealer. One of the local guys Denzel, who had recently been released from prison and was affiliated to the gang, asked if he could come and smoke with me, I agreed, knowing this was the hit but invited him anyway.

I saw when he sat down that he had a knife in his waistband. I had two big bull mastiff dogs and told them to sit in front of him. I told Denzel not to worry and that as long as he did not make any sudden movements the dogs would not attack. I told him that I was going into the main house for a few minutes.

I went into the main house for two hours and watched television, and when I returned saw the two dogs sitting in front of a rather pale Denzel now. Denzel said he wanted to leave, to which I replied that I thought he'd wanted to smoke ... He said that he was feeling rather ill and he just wanted to go home. I walked him out of my yard and have not heard or seen Denzel since.

Andrew and Susan still live in Langebaan. Both of their children have left home. Kendra became a schoolteacher for disabled children and Jared went to hotel school and then went travelling in Europe. Today he works on Luxury Yachts for the rich. Susan still goes to Cape Town five times a week to work, leaving at seven am and returning at seven pm. When Susan gets home from work she cooks, does washing and cleans the house.

On Saturdays she feeds up to fifty street people in the local park using her own money and resources.

She stopped complaining a long time ago, she is a woman of God and will stand by her man in sickness or in health, till death do them part. If she had made another choice, Andrew would be in prison or dead.

Andrew still spends time in his Palace smoking mandrax from seven thirty in the morning till late in the evening; he has dreams of wanting to change the world.

From time to time he would talk about his short spell in prison, and in the end it was not his fault he started using drugs. All he can say is 'I blame the government'.

Jacques

One Act of Kindness saved me

I was born in Johannesburg and raised in a middle class white family. My first memory as a child was of my father beating my mother – and of screaming, drunkenness, fear and the lack of love and affection. My mother had twelve children by four different men. She ran away, taking my sister and I. She soon met another man whom she married and we moved to Kalk Bay, Cape Town.

It was great here but my mother and stepfather were often drunk and I could do what I wanted. I started smoking cigarettes at the age of six. I met a coloured boy named Raymond whose family was extremely poor. I'd often steal food from our house and give it to him. We were soon vandalising cars and homes in our neighbourhood, throwing stones breaking windows and windscreens. One evening we untied all the boats in the harbour. We thought it was the funniest thing as the harbour master ran around trying to tie up some boats as others were floating out of the harbour entrance. I got my first bad beating from my mother that evening with many more to follow. I also upgraded from cigarettes to dagga.

I was seven when I started shoplifting at the local corner store. The owner caught us one day and locked us in the storeroom at the back of the shop until our mothers arrived. We thought we were in heaven and ate as many sweets and drank as much cool drink as we could. That evening the hiding was severe.

My stepbrother and sister were about the same age as my

sister and I, but they were always treated better. On birthdays and Christmas we used to get a puzzle and a packet of sweets, they got bicycles, watches and designer clothes. I was angry about this and promised myself that one day I would return a wealthy man and remind my parents of our treatment as kids.

There was a mental institution down the road from our house. We used to pull faces at the patients, waiting to see their reaction. This got boring after a while and we'd throw stones at the windows until the security chased after us. I now also started sniffing glue when I couldn't get my dagga but it wasn't strong enough and I started smoking mandrax.

I met some older boys who were all seventeen and eighteen and they soon taught me how to break into houses and cars. I used to go and beg for money outside KFC, most times I was given some chicken but I needed money for drugs, and if people didn't give me money I'd swear at them.

When I was eight I met some boys who were in the 26s and others in the 28s. I became a runner, carrying drugs and money for them. I ran away from home and lived in the backyard of a 26, building myself a shack. Whenever I carried drugs, I used to always take a bit for myself. Even at a young age I knew that I had to look out for myself.

Once I stole a handbag which contained R6 500 and a mobile phone. Some members of the 28s gang heard about this and cornered me in an alley. They didn't like me because they knew I ran with the 26s. They stabbed me in my arm and hit me with a machete over the head – I had to get twenty stiches.

We then started stealing mobile phones from school children as they left school. We used to threaten them with a knife or gun. One day I was with one of the older boys after we'd just stolen a young girl's mobile phone. The police were patrolling and thought we were dealing drugs. We were searched and while this was happening a call came over the police radio about the telephone robbery and we were both arrested.

The older youth was nineteen and got five years in jail, I was only ten and was sent to a reformatory inTokai. I was released after two months into my mother's custody. I went back to school and started swimming. I was really good and was asked to join the swimming team. I excelled and soon was beating boys two and three years older than me. Not long after my thirteenth birthday my mother announced that we were moving to the suburb of Landsdowne.

This was the biggest mistake for me, now my life of crime would escalate.

I was placed in a school in Claremont. My school days were boring, we were not taken to swimming classes and there were no other outdoor sports. When we once tried to play football local gangsters stole the ball and some of our trainers. Other times there was intimidation and threats of violence.

I was struggling with lessons and was soon sent to the special class. I thought this was great, because finally the teachers must have realised how special I was. I met a boy called Daniel and soon we were getting up to all sorts of shenanigans.

I was fifteen and now also became aware of my sexuality. We had two friends called Tracy and Pamela who were both fourteen. We would meet in the storeroom after school and have sex. One afternoon while we were having sex with the girls, I heard a shuffle coming from passage and pulled up my pants.

Daniel was still on top of Tracy when the school cleaner burst into the storeroom and we were all caught. The next morning we were all in the principal's office with our parents in tow. Tracy and Pamela's parents wanted to get the police involved but after a long deliberation and the fact that we were all underage, it was decided that the girls would get detention every day for a month and Daniel and I got six of the best each.

I was a bully and I would often beat the younger kids and take their money, the girls were coaxed into having sex. At sixteen I was breaking into shops.

There was a local shop in our neighbourhood run by an old Muslim lady called Aunt Tietie. She was about seventy-five and always worked in the shop during the day, in the evening her son or daughter-in-law used to look after the shop. My friends and I used to steal the refundable bottles from the back of the shop in the yard and then return them to the front for money.

I would distract Aunt Tietie by politely asking for water. She would go to the back of the shop to get it, which took her about five minutes. During that time we helped ourselves to anything we wanted. On her return I would drink the water, say thank you and leave.

One day I once again asked for water and when she went to the back I leant over the counter and stole all the notes out of the till which was about R300. I drank the water thanked her and left. I went and bought some mandrax and alcohol and had a few smokes and drinks, but I felt guilty.

I returned to the shop a few hours later to find her in tears and asked what was wrong. She replied that she had misplaced some money and could not find it and that if her son-in-law arrived and found the money missing then she would be in big trouble. She added that what was worse though, was that she was going to be put into an old age home, but had convinced them that she could earn her keep minding the shop during the day.

I felt really bad and tried everywhere to get some money. I eventually stole a motorbike that evening and sold it to a drug dealer for R500. The following morning I arrived at the shop, but Aunt Tietie was not there, only her son-in-law. I asked him where she was and he said that she was getting too forgetful and that she had lost some money and whenever she worked there were stock discrepancies. He said his wife had found a great home for her where they would be taking her that weekend.

We heard that Aunt Tietie died in the home three months later. She refused to eat and the staff said she lost all the will to live. I never felt so bad or guilty in my life, but I learnt a long time ago that Karma is a bitch and you will pay for your sins in this life, not the next.

I left school and befriended a boy called Jannie, who had five brothers. He was also into housebreaking and soon we were a team. Jannie's mother ran a shebeen and also sold drugs. She was known as Ma Baker. She had old shacks in her backyard where about ten pensioners lived, they all drank and would run a tab with her. She in turn kept their pension books and would cash it in and give them a bit but they were always in her debt. Some were long dead and she would not report this and continue cashing in. When one pensioner died she soon found another to move into his shack.

We befriended a guy called Seal who used to buy rocks from Ma Baker. Seal was a building inspector and would take bribes to pass plans. He always had loads of money and in no time was supporting Jannie and myself. Ma Baker also kept his bank card.

We started running with the gangs and I became known as MacGyver because I could always organise anything – whether it was drugs women or alcohol, or breaking into a house to get goods to sell, then I was the man.

I was caught housebreaking and sent to Tokai reformatory which had become notorious as the worst reformatory in the country. Some gangsters here had already killed and here was where I learnt about fear and how to rule by fear.

If you were from outside the Western Cape you were severely beaten. I was okay and already knew a lot of the offenders here. There were only two wardens for five hostels in the evening and it took them approximately one and a half hours to complete a round, this gave us a lot of time to get up to no good.

New recruits were inducted into a game called Bingo. Six of the new recruits were put in a circle and each given a biscuit. When they

85

all had to masturbate and ejaculate on their biscuit when finished you had to shout Bingo and the last person to shout Bingo had to eat all six semen-soaked biscuits. If any of the new recruits refused to play he was severely beaten with soap in socks by the older intakes. We once beat a boy so hard that his one testicle dislodged and moved. When the wardens arrived, he was unconscious and taken to hospital where he spent the next few days.

One of the overseers saw that I was a good worker and gave me a job cleaning his property. I found five litres of thinners in his shed and would fill an empty shampoo bottle and take it to my dormitory. I'd then soak a cloth in it, sniffing for an instant buzz and sharing with my friends. My overseer noticed a few weeks later that he only had about one litre of thinners left and I lost my job.

I then had to slog with the rest of the guys in the vineyard where the work was much harder. I found a weed known to contain malpitte (Datura stramonium). It is also a powerful hallucinogen which is used for the intense visions it produces. Datura is also used as a herbal medicine to relieve asthma and other illnesses. Slightly higher amounts are toxic and careless use often results in death and hospitalisation.

If you took about ten of these seeds it was like an LSD trip. I sold these for R5 for a full matchbox. Some of the guys were tripping for three days. They would crawl on all fours in the classroom and play with the teachers shoelaces, others would strip down to their underpants, saying they have to get ready for work, while others would laugh and cry at the same time, others would have deep conversations with plants and rocks.

I got ratted out by one of the younger recruits after he urinated on a teacher's leg while tripping. I got six of the best and was transferred to a reformatory in Dewetsdorp, Bloemfontein.

I was taken to the airport at five am the following morning, but on the way to the airport we got side swiped by another car, which smashed into the passenger side where I was sitting. We continued our trip to the airport where my parents came to see me off. I was crying, saying that I was in pain and needed a doctor. My teacher and parents said that I had to get on the plane and get medical attention when I reached my destination.

When I arrived in Bloemfontein there was nobody to meet me, I had some money and hobbled along looking for a dealer.

It is always easy to find a dealer no matter which city in the world. The best way is to find a Rastafarian – they can always point you in the right direction. I bought some weed, had a smoke and then made my way back to the airport. I met the teacher who was looking for me. We then made our way to Dewetsdorp.

Tokai reformatory had a bad reputation. Dewetsdorp did not, but I was now a small fish in a big pond. I was the outsider from the Western Cape and these guys would definitely try and make things very difficult for me.

One of the boys, an Afrikaner named Gerhart who was about six foot and weighed close to one hundred and twenty kilograms, escorted to my new dorm. I met a few of the boys and they asked if I had any weed. I said I did and we all had a joint. Gerhart returned and said I had to go outside with him.

I was warned by all in my dormitory that he was a bully. Outside a big group of boys had already gathered. Gerhart said he was going to throw me into a pile of horse manure nearby. I noticed that he had two scars on his nose from a recent operation.

As he approached me I hit him with all my strength square on the nose. Blood shot in all directions and he collapsed to the ground screaming in pain. I carried him to my bed and someone called the matron. I explained to her that the boys were trying to initiate me and that I had struck out. All the boys wanted to know who had beaten the bully. I gained respect from everyone that day. Gerhart spend a week in hospital and on his return was very apologetic.

One of the classes I attended was in spray-painting. The teacher of the class said to me that I was there not to fight but to learn, and asked whether I'd done any spray painting in the past.

I had helped a friend in his panel beating shop a few years previously and had learnt the art. I said that I had. He then proceeded to hand out exam papers to the class, and asked if I wanted to do the test. I said yes. I knew all the answers and finished the test before anyone else. I got full marks. The teacher gave us a practical exam the next day and once again I excelled. He then asked me to come and work at the workshop at his house where he restored cars as a hobby. He paid me R200 a week.

There was a drug merchant living a few houses from where he lived and I was buying marijuana and selling it back at the reformatory. After a few months the work dried up and so did the marijuana.

There was a one hundred and fifty litre drum of thinners in the workshop. I would go in through a window I left open at the end of the working day, and steal thinners every night and then have a party of note with the guys back at the dormitory.

After a few weeks the drum had less than one hundred litres left. One evening, after sniffing huge amounts of thinners, the guys asked me to go and get more. I climbed through the window. It was very dark and I was high. I stood over the drum and could not get the cap off so I lit my lighter to see what was going on and the drum caught alight.

I ran away and waited not far from the workshop. The next moment the drum shot through the asbestos roof and the whole workshop was on fire. I was the prime suspect and a few of us were questioned by the police in the headmaster's office. There were a few guys, well known for ratting on people, who were called in before me. There was a queue of about ten boys and after the first boy came out after two minutes the policeman said Jacques come in here. He just looked at me and said 'I know it was you now tell me what happened'.

I was locked up in the local police cells for two days then appeared before the magistrate where I was found guilty and sent for seven cuts by the police with a cane. I knew about six of the best handed out by teachers and I knew this was going to be bad. There were two other boys on different charges, who also were also to receive seven cuts each the next day.

The first boy went in and when I heard him screaming after the first hit I pissed in my pants. I said to the other boy that I would go next because I wanted to get it over with. In the middle of the room was a wooden chair, I was told to sit down and crouch, then my hands were tied to a bar in front of the chair and a thin blanket was placed over my kidneys, it was the most excruciating pain I had ever experienced. After the third hit, the policeman said that if I did not scream he would hit me in quick succession for the remaining four cuts. I could hardly walk and could not sit in the car on the drive back to the reformatory and lay on my side. I was booked of school for a week and I was black and blue, I still have a scar from one of the cuts to this day.

I behaved as much as I could from that day on and on my eighteenth birthday I was sent home. I was not welcome at home and moved into one of my 26s friend's home. I got back into my old ways as I could not find work no matter how hard I tried. I started housebreaking once again.

One day my coloured friend Jakkels and I were on a bicycle, I was giving him a lift on the handle bars. We passed two men and a girl and they made some comment and started laughing. I attacked the one guy and Jakkels beat up the other guy. We took off their trainers and threw them over a nearby bridge. We got on the bicycle and got on our way. Twenty minutes later we were arrested by the police and I then found out that while Jakkels had been beating the boy he also stole his watch, gold chain and cash. We now not only had an assault charge but one for theft as well.

Jakkels was only seventeen and was released into his mother's custody. I got bailed for R500. A few months later at our court appearance, Jakkels was sentenced to six cuts and I got five years in jail.

I was initially in the holding cells in Wynberg, known as Die Gat (The Hole). The cells can accommodate thirty men but there were always more than sixty men in the cell at any given time. New prisoners suffered horroffic abuse here.

When a new offender arrived he would have all goods taken from him including his shoes or trainers from the numbers that run the cell. They would tell the man to lift his head, exposing his neck, and then punch with full force to the jugular, rendering the person unconscious for a few seconds. As soon as he is awake again the whole process is repeated. Then you are told to lift your head and to blow up one cheek, you then get punched on this cheek and this would also render you unconscious for a few seconds. This is the beginning, where you are showed the numbers strength and how the rule by fear.

In the toilet area in the corner of the cell some of the numbers would be making Koole – marijuana in plastic sheeting about seven inches long and two inches thick. This is burned and sealed at both ends with a lighter. It is then covered in spit and forced up the new prisoner's anus, telling him to smuggle it into Pollsmoor. The 26s deal in money, anything that shines and that has value; the 27s deal in blood and are enforcers; the 28s in sex and tobacco.

All police and warders can be bought and I witnessed both police and wardens exchanging cigarettes, marijuana and drugs for cash. Some of the weaker men get raped by the 28s and the police and wardens just turn a blind eye. Some more experienced prisoners can carry mobile phones in their anuses and I once saw a man insert Koole the size of a peanut butter bottle. Then you get transferred to Pollsmoor in vans, where new prisoners also have all their valuables taken from them and are sometimes raped.

By the time we arrived at Pollsmoor there were many complaints but Wardens don't listen and say they will investigate but never do.

Franse have to carry the most contraband. Everyone is strip searched to check for contraband and also for tattoos to check gang affiliation. Often contraband is found and sometimes it is not even the prisoners goods, as he was forced to carry it in. He then gets charged with this offence. The wardens do not care unless someone is murdered. Then everyone gets processed, there is lots of paperwork and prisoners help with this. These are the prisoners that get given the contraband not found. This is in turn distributed to the cells it was intended for. They get paid in cash, pills or some marijuana, for their part in this.

The first cell that all new prisoners sleep in is called Die Hof Kamer (The Court Room). This cell is once again meant to accommodate twenty-five prisoners but most of the time between fifty and sixty prisoners can be found here. There are no bunks here and only mattresses and blankets on the floor. It is so packed that you sometimes can only sleep on your side.

The 26s and 27s sleep on the right of the room and the 28s sleep on the left, the Franse sleep in the centre of the room on the floor, known as Die Bos (The Bush). It's filthy. There are vagrants who sleep next to you as well as lice and cockroaches. And it stinks, keeping in mind there's one toilet for sixty men.

On arrival here all the Franse are told to go to the Die Bos, strip and place all their clothes in the middle. One man from each camp searches the clothes for any valuables, cigarettes or drugs. Some men sew contraband into the seams of their clothes and others tie rolled up contraband to a piece of cotton and tie one end to a tooth and swallow, for retrieval later. If anything is found on you by any of the camps you get beaten.

I had been running with the 26s before I arrived in prison so I was a 26s Frans, which meant I worked for them but I did not take the number. I had do mostly the risky and dirty work for the 26s.

When I arrived in the cell they gave me a couple of joints and told me to go and lie in Die Bos. Later that evening the man next to me tapped me on the shoulder and said that a 28 was calling me over, I was terrified and knew that this man wanted sex. I went over to him, he said come sit by me and I sat on the edge of his mattress. He was scary looking and had tattoos all over his face.

He said to me 'Jou ma se poes, ek sal you gesiggie gou lelik maak', (your mothers vagina, I will make your face ugly very quickly). He then lifted the blanket, exposing his erect penis, with a minora blade and a toothbrush with a spike lying on top of his stomach. He wanted to instill fear so that I'd submit. I jumped up and said loudly, 'I am not in your camp but with the 26s'.

All the 26s got fully dressed shoes, boots and scarves to cover their necks to protect against being stabbed. They stick up their thumb with their first two fingers together, which means a 26 is approaching and the two camps approach each other.

They speak Sabela and say things like what is your name, what are you doing here and where do you live. When there is a dispute between a 26 and 28 it has to be sanctioned for battle, otherwise discussed or this can mean war between the numbers.

This was not the first complaint against this 28. You only get three warnings by your number and then the number court punishment is dealt out. When back in normal prison population sentence is usually handed down.

Blankets are placed in a circle of six bunks at the end of the cell, so that no one can see what is going on. The offender sits in the middle and the punishers form a circle around him, the highest ranking of a number will observe and keep count and to start the punishment and say 'Ups' if a 26, 'Hons' if a 27 and 'why' if a 28. After the punishment this is repeated.

There are three different punishments handed down. The first

92

form of punishment is a beating with soap in socks. So if there are 6 number 28s in a cell, each has to hit the offender twenty-eight times. The same if you are a 26 which is twenty-six hits and 27 get twenty-seven hits each. With a stroke of good luck there may only be three or four of the number handing down the punishment in the cell, at other times there could be as many as sixteen.

The second punishment is steel cups hooked to a belt and the third is locks hooked to a belt which can be any lock size available.

The soap will make a man black and blue, the steel cup often gives deep gashes and cuts, the locks break bones makes massive holes in skulls and more often than not this ends in hospitalisation.

After the punishment the Ngangi or numbers Doctor will check the damage and ash is rubbed into small cuts, bigger cuts of two inches or more will get bandaged, if it is worse a warden is called, When the warden arrives they will say that the man fell. The prison doctor can clearly see that this was a beating but knows that it is pointless making a report as the victim rarely tells.

Sometimes a Frans will be given this punishment but only after three or four warnings. Some men will sit and hold their heads and take the punishment, others would jump around as they are hit and you would have to duck under your bunk or also be in the firing line. When I used to see the blankets been hung, I'd wrap three blankets around me and get out of harm's way.

Then you are allocated a cell, which once again would be overpopulated. Here the men who had Koole inserted in their anuses are told to remove it. This often breaks up and leaks and depending on the contents can make a prisoner severely ill.

It sometimes get stuck and I have seen numbers jump on a man's stomach in the hope that it is excreted, if this does not work then a toothbrush is used that has been burnt at the end and turned into a hook. They then try and pull it out, damaging your insides in the process. This often leads to hospitalisation and if the Koole is still inside you, you get charged.

93

There are three ways to survive in prison: the first is to join a number, two is to pay money into a numbers property for protection, and thirdly you can ask to be moved to a single cell that usually sleeps three. There are also cells for Muslims and Christians.

I was a Frans's 26 and knew two merchants who wanted to use me, so I was placed in a single cell with two other men. On my second day a warden arrived and handed me ninety-six bankies of Marijuana, five hundred madrax tablets and R3 000 cash in a paper bag.

Wardens get paid by the 15th of a month, so by the 25th they were broke. Their low wages made it easy to bribe them. I would ask another warden to see the chaplain/doctor/therapist, which would give me twenty minutes to distribute the contraband between the 26s cells. I would get some marijuana or mandrax as payment, this I would sell but keep a bit for my own use. I saw more money and drugs in prison than on the outside. Wardens would go to dealers on the outside to get drugs and money, many wardens have addiction problems.

I learnt the art of tattoos in prison and we would use the tools available to us.

I was particularly skilled and did not do your rough standard prison tattoo and was in demand, once tattooing a warden's arm through my cells broken pane window over a two day period for R200. We used plastic seals that people often wear as bracelets and burn it until it turns into ash, then we'd use spit and turn it into a paste, this was the ink.

We'd take two matchsticks and insert two thin needles, if there were no needles, we used staples ground down on a brick with spit to a thin sharp point. Then it gets dipped in the ink and tapped on the skin deep enough to draw blood, over a thin outline of the tattoo drawn with a pen.

I used to boil water for tea or coffee, because there were no kettles, by tying a toothbrush handle between two spoons then

94

placing an electrical wire to the end of each spoon. I'd then plug it in and place it in a plastic bowl filled with water, the water took about fifteen minutes to boil.

We also used the 'prison telephone' to communicate with inmates in other cells if mobile phones were not available. So let's say you arranged to talk at eight pm then you would empty your toilet and dry it with a towel, he would do the same. Then you can talk into the toilet and thus communicate this way, no one else can hear you, even if the other toilet is twenty cells away.

Another way to communicate is by 'long arm'. You tear up a sheet into strips, then tie to the length you need. This can be done up to ten metres. Then you tie a shoe to the end of the length, the other person sticks out his leg or arm and then you swing it until you have enough momentum then fling it until it wraps around his arm or leg, this way you can exchange anything.

I would get someone to pay money into my property. I would tell them to pay R100 into my property and R100 on the chef's property. Then I take my R100 and go the leader of the cell and ask for tobacco and chocolate. He will give you a little tobacco and half a chocolate; you have to share this with your fellow Franse. I have now arranged with the chef to get me a roast chicken.

Some prisoners are fed in their cells so he would hide the chicken that he had previously cooked at the bottom of the food container where the warm water is kept to keep the food hot. When he passes my cell he would slip it to me, I would end up with one piece of chicken after sharing.

When I was in a single cell I once again started living up to my name MacGyver. Here I arranged twenty five kilogram bags of sugar, powder milk and even a radio. Now to get twenty five kilograms through a cell opening never created a problem and in prison you become very creative. I would have an empty bag and let it be poured in until the other bag was thin enough to squeeze through the bars. I did two and a half years of my sentence and was released – six months later I was convicted of housebreaking and theft and sent to Pollsmoor for nine years.

There were young prison wardens who wanted to become numbers and would spend a lot of time with the Captains and the Generals. They used these officers to smuggle drugs, money, and whatever was needed in and out of prison for them. In return they gave them information on the number but not everything. The prison officer would then speak to other numbers and earn respect, because he has knowledge on the number.

I was put in a single cell after a few years; this cell was also used by prison officers to leave their batons and spare uniforms. I gained their trust and never touched any of their stuff.

There was a cell opposite me with fifty men and the leader of this cell was a 28s General called Kale. He approached me in the exercise yard one day and asked if I could keep something in my cell for him, as he'd had word that his cell was being raided. I agreed, and he'd reiterated to me that I not give it to anyone other than himself, no matter who asked.

There was a man who walked with a bucket of spoons and handed them out before the three pm meal and then collected it afterwards. When he got to Kale's cell, Kale put a plastic shopping bag in the bucket and said, 'Quick get that to Jacques'.

The bag was handed to me and it felt quite heavy, later that evening my curiosity got the better of me and I opened the bag slowly, checking for knots. Sometimes there is a seal made with a lighter, just big enough to notice if the bag had been opened. There was a bag within a bag within a bag.

I was shocked when I discovered what was inside: R3 500 in cash, a big bag of dagga, about sixty mandrax pills, eight knives, two 9mm guns and a limpet mine! I had a washing line in my cell a bit higher than I was tall. I took a jacket, put the knives, guns, drugs and money in the one sleeve and the limpet mine in the other, sealed the sleeves at the ends so that it was not noticeable and hung it over the washing line. I had off course helped myself to some marijuana, just enough so that it would not be missed.

The passage light between the cells was on twenty-four hours a day. Two days later, at twelve thirty in the morning the lights went out for five minutes. There was scuffling and then I could year the cell opposite me being opened. The lights went on and there were about twenty task force members wearing full combat gear and balaclavas so that if a prisoner got killed or injured then the officer could not be identified – often in raids like these, prisoners would end up with broken bones.

They stormed the cell and five minutes later marched all the guys outside into the passage, stripped them naked and then proceeded to give all the men a cavity search (inserting a gloved finger into the anus, to search for contraband). I knew that there must have been a snitch, because Kale was the only person taken away and put in Medium B section in a single cell with a twenty-four hour guard, and no contact with anyone.

I knew that if I got caught with this stuff then I would get a very long sentence, but if I pimped (snitched) the consequences would be worse. After about twenty days two 28s from Kales cell approached me and said they knew I had the stuff and to hand it to them.

I told them that Kale had told me in no uncertain terms that I was not to give it to anyone, and besides I had given it to a warden for safekeeping on the outside. My cell was not searched because the officers had goods in my cell and nothing ever went missing. One month and a day later Kale was brought back to the main population. He had been beaten and interrogated, he denied any knowledge and it was assumed that an officer must have smuggled it out of prison.

While he was waiting to be put in his cell he turned around and gave me an evil stare. He told me I'd probably got rid of the stuff.

'I am a man of honesty, I have your stuff' I replied. He said 'Jy praat kak my bru' (you are talking shit bro). He said I'd taken a big chance because if I'd been caught, I would have died in prison. He also said 'Jy is a whitie, maar net die waarheid' (you are a white man of truth). Then a prison officer interrupted us.

Later in the yard I went to Kale who was with the two 28s who had asked for the stuff, and I said in front of them I wouldn't give it to anyone but Kale. The two 28s confirmed this. I did not pimp them but knew they were bitter now, knowing I'd had the stuff all the time. When the spoon man came around we followed the same procedure. They checked if everything was there and half an hour later Kale spoke to me through the cells and said 'I can testify that you are my brother, anything you ever need do not hesitate to ask'. Later he sent over R200, two mandrax tablets and a bankie of dagga. Because of this the rest of my time in prison became easier.

I was transferred to a prison in Helderstroom not long after because it was suspected that I had the goods in question, but nothing could be proven. I told Kale that I was being transferred and he did some investigating. He found out that the transfer document had another prisoner's name scratched out and replaced with mine. This was illegal but the transfer still took place.

When I arrived at Helderstroom one of the prisoners approached me in reception and asked if I was Jacques. I said I was, he had my name and prison number written on the back of his hand. I did not have to complete any documentation and was taken straight to a cell where I was shown a bed with a great mattress and told that I would be looked after here and if I ever needed or wanted anything I just had to ask.

Life was a lot easier. On Christmas day we all got a quarter chicken, potatoes, rice and salad. I was in my cell and feeling quite satisfied after smoking a joint, when I noticed a silver twenty-five litre drum placed outside my cell door. I asked what it was and was told that it was ice cream, a gift from an inmate's wife. She had given thirty cells this gift of ice cream. This was a great Christmas and I decided that I would track down the inmate the following day and thank him.

I found out that the inmate was called Shaque and tracked down his cell which housed fifty people and off course was overcrowded. I was stopped at the cell door and asked what I wanted by a numbers soldier, I asked to see Shaque and I was told to wait while another soldier took over the post. I was told that Shaque would see me.

When I got half way into the cell I noticed that it was cordoned off with blankets. I knew that it was unheard of for a frans to go beyond this point and it was only meant for senior members of the gang. When I passed through the blankets I could not believe my eyes, there were leather seats, tables, duvets and there was a table full of cash, dagga and other drugs.

Shaque said from the table where he was counting some money 'Whitie wat soek jy?' (white man what do you want)? I said that I had heard it was his wife who'd bought all the prisoners ice cream. He replied now a bit more agitated 'Wat de fok het dit met jou uit te maak' (What the fuck has it got to do with you)? I now became afraid because all his men stepped closer and were Britished (ready for battle).

I told Shaque 'I just wanted to thank you' He turned to all his men and said this is the only person in the whole prison that has thanked me, not even you my men. Shaque is the kind of man your mother always warned you about.

He asked me if I smoked dagga and I said I did, he asked if I had any money, I said none. He told me I had good manners and then gave me, some tobacco, dagga and R200 and added that if I ever needed anything to come and see him. I was afraid of him and asked if I could leave. He said before you leave you have not seen anything and what is about to happen.

As I turned around to walk away a soldier came at me with a blade. I froze, I felt the thumb on my chest and urinated in my pants.

I looked down to see the wound and realised that he had turned the knife around and hit me with the handle, everyone was laughing, Shaque said this was my warning and that I hadn't seen anything. I was relieved to get out the cell. I never went back to the cell.

I always saw Shaque in the exercise yard smoking a joint openly. He called me over one day and all his men were around him. He told me to sit down and I sat a half a metre away on a crate. He leaned over, pulled me closer and said 'Jacques are you afraid of me'? I replied yes and he asked why I hadn't asked him for anything. He asked if I needed anything. I said I needed toiletries. He instructed a soldier to go with me to his cupboard and told me to get what I needed.

I avoided Shaque but he would from time to time give me dagga, money and drugs and ask for nothing in return. I got a job in the warden's mess hall and this proved to be very lucrative. On many weekends wardens would come to me and say: 'Here is R100, I am braaing (BBQ) tonight.' I would take their car keys while he or she was having lunch, go to the fridge and get them a mixture of the best cuts of meat and put it into the boot of their car and return the keys.

I did a lot of smuggling from the kitchen and mess but four months before I was up for parole I stopped all activities.

I got paroled one day early and when I got to Cape Town station there was nobody to meet me. I took another train and before I took my seat bumped into my sister. She could not believe it and asked why I was a day early.

I was reunited with my mother later that day and not long after got a job as a carpenter. The next two years were great and I was never happier until my mother died and a few weeks later I was retrenched.

I could not get work because of my criminal background and ended up on the streets of Cape Town for the next five years begging for enough money daily to buy a bit of food and some alcohol to sleep warmly at night in the local park.

I was begging at my favourite spot in town at the traffic lights one day when I noticed a girl of about twenty at the office block across the road on the first floor, crying.

At first I did nothing but then I realised she was looking at me. I felt shame and embarrassment and walked around the corner where I stayed for about ten minutes. I returned to the traffic lights and made sure that the girl was not there. I continued begging and suddenly I felt a tap on my shoulder.

Here was the girl who handed me a can of Coca Cola and five rand and said 'it is not much but it is all I have'. I felt ashamed and the next day went to a local church and asked where I could get help. I was directed to Elpetra ministries, which is a working farm for rehabilitated gangsters and addicts. I spent six months here and turned my life around.

I went to Cape Town after three months looking for this girl. I went to the office block and asked her colleagues where the girl was who had helped the beggar who used to beg at the traffic lights. They said they'd all wondered what had happened to him, I said I am that man, and they couldn't believe it. They asked me to wait in an office as the girl would be back in five minutes.

When she returned her colleagues told her that someone was there to see her. She walked into the room sat down and asked how she could help me. I asked if she could remember the beggar who used to beg at the traffic lights, she said she did and asked what had happened to him. I said that man has changed his life around, he does not drink and has found God, but he would like to thank you for your act of kindness because it was you who changed and saved his life.

Jacques said there was one more thing 'I am that man'. She burst into tears and so did I. We stay in touch now and I see her when I can.

Her name is Francine. My life was saved by her act of kindness.

101

Ronald

Please don't divorce me daddy

I was born into a family of seven siblings – six girls and myself. My father longed for a son and was going to give up after number seven. He was a furniture salesman for a company owned by an elderly Greek woman. My earliest memory was of this kind woman telling me that she'd pray for me. We were struggling to make ends meet and barely had enough food on the table, but our family was always close. My father shot himself when I was five years old. My sisters were wowed by material things local gangsters were able to offer. My sister Geraldine married a 27s General called Nazeer, who was a Muslim. Nazeer soon took me under his wing, becoming a father figure. I respected him and he showered my sister and I with gifts. He bought me a horse for my seventh birthday.

Nazeer had a farm in Stellenbosch, where most drug deals were done and the drugs kept. The drugs were hidden under Rottweiler cages at the back of the house and under the chicken coups. I saw bucket loads of drugs. There were lots of men who used to come and go and many had guns that they let me play with. Once a man handed Nazeer a suitcase full of mandrax, and I said to him 'Naz can I have some sweeties', to which he replied 'No Ronnie, these you smoke'.

Business was booming and soon the empire had expanded to Paarl and Ceres where Nazeer would give the farm labourers drugs in exchange for stolen fruit and vegetables. The fruit was then sold at market stalls, along with drugs. Lots of men who were recently released from prison worked for Nazeer. Outside of prison a 26 appears as a 27 but this is just a mask.

Nazeer had a 26 enforcer called Jasper who came from Durban and was the leader of the Jakkies gang. I use to go with Jasper and Nazeer on collections. If a dealer was short on payment, then Jasper would beat him with his weapon of choice, which was a spade. Nazeer also had many shopkeepers around the Cape Peninsula in his pocket; giving them loans on condition that he could sell drugs from their premises. Everyone working for Nazeer knew that they could be replaced at any time if they stepped out of line.

I used to play with the children whose fathers worked for Nazeer. One afternoon one of my friend's fathers was brought to the farm and was beaten to death in the shower. Nazeer told me that is what happened when people didn't listen. I was nine and a half years old.

Another time I saw a man on his knees in the stables – he was shot in the back of the head. I was told he didn't want to listen either. I was ten when I witnessed my second killing. Many men disappeared and I was told that they were gone forever.

A few days after my twelfth birthday I was taught and soldiered into the number and was learning to speak Sabela. I was taught discipline and respect but only for those in my 'family'.

The first rule was never sell drugs from where you live. There was lots of cash around and many times I saw black bin liners full of cash wrapped in bundles. Nazeer bought me a motorbike for my thirteenth birthday. Nazeer's motto was 'what will be, will be'. He was a bad man but believed in God.

My sister Janine was clubbing a lot and one evening she came home drunk. I slapped her in the face and told her to behave herself. I told Nazeer what had happened and he went outside to confront the boys who'd just dropped her off but they were gone. The following evening the same thing happened, we ran outside and fired shots at their car and they all ran away, we then set their car alight. We weren't concerned about the police because we had lots of policeman on our payroll and as I learned from a young age, any policeman can be bought.

I joined the Americans gang when I was fifteen. We were called the YA (Young Americans). Most of the older boys were nineteen and twenty, I controlled the younger guys and we regularly got involved in gang fights.

We were going to fight some of the Hard Livings, when one of our boys said he didn't want to go. If your brothers tell you to join them to do anything you have to, that is the way of gangs. I stabbed the boy and cut out his gang tattoo, he died in hospital but he managed to stab me and I ended up in hospital for a month.

I was sent to Pollsmoor's juvenile section and lots of the boys there my age were numbers. In prison, gang affiliation doesn't matter – only the number rules here.

Here I was tested. Numbers would tell you things like you had nice eyes for example, and if you said thanks or acted coy, then you got beaten or raped, you had to stand up for yourself and fight. I was taken under the wing of a 27 and was schooled in the way of the number 27. I always had drugs in prison and one day one of the new intakes asked me for some marijuana in exchange for sex. I spoke to him nicely and told him that here not everyone had sex with each other. I warned him that some of the men would have sex with you, then cut and stab you afterwards. I gave him some weed. After two years I was released.

I started dealing drugs in Sea Point at the clubs. It was mostly coke and ecstasy. We fought the Hard Livings on many occasions for this turf – this was where all the yuppies and rich kids use to hang out. I had my own crew and we stole cars and bought drugs and sold it for massive profits.

I went to Frans's homes whom I looked out for in prison, and told them they had to repay their debt. I had an enforcer called

Ali. He was fearless and would kill whenever I gave the order. We would go to a Frans's house and demand he look after two guns for me, drink all his all his alcohol, use his drugs and then call the woman over. I found those women were easy when you had drugs and would do anything.

I was using more drugs than ever before and was becoming irrational. Nazeer came to fetch me and sat me down and told me to calm things down as I was drawing a lot of unwanted attention.

He sent me to one of his drug houses in Mitchell's Plain to oversee and look after the money for him. The woman of the house, Jolene, was thirty and had two small kids. Nazeer told her to tell him how much drugs I used. Her husband was in prison and I used to send him money from what we made.

Soon I was having sex with Jolene and when Nazeer asked her what I was doing and taking, she would lie for me. Her husband came out of prison and I told him that as I'd looked after him and his family, he could live with his brother and I'd tell him when he could visit. I had a fierce reputation and he didn't argue. I gave him some drugs to sell from his brother's and a few months later, his brother stabbed him to death. The way I was living was like the movies, I had money, women, nice clothes and a flashy car. I was eighteen.

In those days the Americans, who also fought against the Vultures and the Genuines who had an affiliation, started fighting over drug turf in Hanover Park.

I was at one of our dens where we were having a big party. I smoked some buttons and then decided to smoke some rocks. This was the first time I had smoked rocks and I went and sat at the front door to get some fresh air. I saw three guys who were from the Vultures walk past and I fired three shots after them.

A few hours later the party moved to the bedrooms where we were having sex. My friend was on a single bed in the corner of the room with his woman and I was on the double bed with mine. We heard a loud bang and realised that the front door was being broken down. We thought it was a drug bust and the girl of the house, Jane, threw the drug stash down the shaft at the back of the toilet. There was a Christian woman who lived a floor below and she would look after the drugs in exchange for money.

It was about forty men and boys from the Vultures gang, they stormed into the room and hit my friend over the head with a hammer, one of the guys stabbed me thru the arm and pinned me to the bed. One of the guys recognised me and said to the rest of the guys that I was an American captain and that I should be Dalad (Sabela for kill).

The girls pushed the men out the room, they could not kill us because it meant that they would have to kill the girls as well. I went to hospital where we got stitched up.

I told the nurses 'I was just finished with the tits and was about to do the deed when these gangsters broke in'. Some other Americans arrived and I told them that we must take revenge. They told me to wait until I was better but I told them no. I pulled out my 9mm and left the hospital. We cruised round the area in a few cars and saw a group of Vultures standing on a street corner. I shot wildly into the crowd, wounding a few. I later heard that one of the guys had been paralysed from the waist down and would never walk again.

I decided to go home to the farm. I hadn't seen Nazeer for a few months and did not know how he would react. When he saw me, he hugged me and said that he hoped I had learned my lesson. I felt like the return of the prodigal son. I got away with a lot more than others with him.

He asked me if I was still smoking mandrax and I said no, only slow boats (joints). He caught me having a mandrax pipe in the stables on day and said to me God was watching. I couldn't understand why this gangster had so much faith.

I went to church with Geraldine and saw that church was where all the beautiful women hung out. I met a nice girl named Gillian and we started dating, she was the love of my life and the one that got away.

I took her to the Galaxy nightclub for a Saturday matinee. She saw that all the girls danced with me and that I was very popular. My sister Janine who still had a grudge after all these years after I slapped her, told Gillian who I was and what I had done, Gillian left me and I never spoke to Janine for ten years.

I was looking after a General Isaac from the Americans's wife while he was in prison. She was a twin and I married her sister Maxi, then moved to Kraaifontein where I started dealing again.

When Isaac was released from prison he gave me a house, a new car and guns and asked me to work with him. I agreed. The police didn't know much about me, but one afternoon they pulled me over and said that they knew who I was, what I did and that if I worked undercover for them, they would turn a blind eye.

This was a great opportunity because now I could show the police just where my opposition was operating.

We also started moving drugs into prison because this was much more lucrative and we could make five times more money than on the outside. We would meet a prison guard in a shopping centre car park and hand him five hundred mandrax pills. He in turn would hand us R50 000 in cash. We were soon also dealing in other prisons. We would buy three thousand mandrax tablets a week, sell a thousand from the den and send two thousand into prisons.

We also sold five hundred packets of tik at R30 each a day – a R30 bag is about half the size of a peanut. I had too much money and would pay it into different family member's accounts. My cousin used to smoke buttons so I use to deposit R100 000 into his account a week and give him R500 and five buttons.

We also used to get lots of stolen goods. Junkies would bring us a R2 000 camera and we would give them two R30 bags that only cost us about R5. Other times I would give girls one bag for a blowjob or full sex. I had a lawyer who bought ten R30 bags a time; I sold it to him for R500.

I met a man from the Transkei who used to bring me huge bags of marijuana and sell it to me for R1 000, I sold these for between R50 000 and R100 000. He us to meet me in a KFC car park, we used to then exchange car keys and once I had delivered the goods I'd return his car.

I met him one day at KFC again and he gave me a bag of yellow powder which was an oil-based tik. He told me to go and try it in the toilets to see if I was interested. I always had a lolly on me and went to the toilets and had one hit. When I came out my friend said 'Yo Bro, your eyes are like saucers and you are chewing your jaw'. I said it was the best shit I had ever had.

The deal was fifty/ fifty, he agreed. I took the stuff to Nazeer but kept half for myself. Nazeer got his top smoker and told him to try it out. He took one hit and said it was good stuff. Nazeer told us to rob the guy. I said no, telling him I'd been buying marijuana from him for a long time. Nazeer then wanted to meet him, but I said the guy was afraid of him. This was a lie because then I would be cut out of the deal.

We started cutting and weighing the new drug at my house and while we were doing this we were partying and giving the girls around us some in exchange for sex, off course. One of Nazeer's captains was told to watch us and he reported back to Nazeer.

Nazeer approached me and said I'd been neglecting my wife. I went to my wife and told her I was leaving. Now I was seeing my daughters only every second weekend. I arrived one day and my five-year-old daughter asked why we didn't eat together anymore. She looked into my eyes gave me a huge hug and said 'Daddy please don't divorce me'. My heart was in my throat and I struggled to hold back the tears.

I decided that day that I'd check into Elpetra ministry which is a

Christian rehab on a working farm for six months. I was sent home for a week after the first month for smoking dope on the farm. I felt ashamed that I had let my kids down.

I returned and after a short while the pastor approached me and asked me to be a leader. I said I couldn't because at this point I did not surrender to God completely. He replied that I could start by leading, I asked to be baptized. It was a rainy cold Sunday and freezing cold when about nine of the disciples at the school and I were driven to the beach to get baptized.

I could not believe why such a day had to be picked, I was kneeling in the surf and the water reached my chest, waves were splashing over me. The pastor said a prayer, then put my head under the water briefly, when I surfaced the sun came out, the sky cleared and I was warm! I was running up and down the beach like a child and had never felt so at peace and free in my life. I accepted Jesus Christ as my Lord and Saviour that day.

I had a thirty a day cigarette habit and stopped a week later. I went home to visit my wife, whom I reconciled with.

I called my sister whom I hadn't spoken to for ten years and asked her forgiveness.

I want to be a father and husband and show others that there is a way out. I saw Nazeer and told him that I had given my life to the lord and that I was turning away from the life of crime. He took out a wad of cash but I said 'No thank you, I do not want your blood money'. He said I'd be back. I said 'Naz what will be will be, I will pray for you', because I will never forget the day my daughter said 'Please don't divorce me daddy'.

Bob

Your darkest hour only last sixty minutes

I was born in Alloa Scotland and had one sister. I had a privileged upbringing and got everything a boy could want. I left school and started my own business buying and selling cars. I started a few other businesses and soon was earning a small fortune. My grandparents went on holiday to South Africa one year, fell in love with the place and decided to stay. My parents followed, so did my aunt, uncle and cousins. I had a long-term girlfriend but she didn't want to live in South Africa. A few years later we split up so I sold my businesses and moved to South Africa.

I moved to Cape Town to be near my parents and other family members. I started my own business and was doing extremely well. I had a few girlfriends but nobody that rocked my world.

Then I met a beautiful woman called Grace, we fell in love and moved in together. Every second weekend her ex-husband would collect her kids to stay at his house, so we would take off and have dirty weekends in the wine lands. We also fell in love with the area. Then we took a holiday abroad and on our return decided to look for a house in the wine lands.

We scoured the weekend newspaper and looked at houses in that area and we packed our bags and went off for another romantic weekend. We contacted an estate agent when we arrived in the area.

We were going to buy a plot but the second house we looked at had thirty metre high trees with large grounds and it was stunning. We both fell in love with the place instantly and within three hours of our break had bought this R3 million property and taken a R30 000 a month bond even though our current house had not even been put on the market yet.

Eight months later we sold our house and moved to the new house, which was only a barn at the time with a cottage at the bottom of the garden. We knocked down the main house and built a new house. There was so much noise that we rented another house during the construction of the new place.

The builder fell way behind. We had been paying a weekly fee and now we were over by R450 000 of what was due. The builder walked off site and we later found out that he had also stolen R280 000 from our building supplier. I tried to hide this from Grace and I started to stress. This was when I was introduced to tik.

My business was booming and I was earning between R80 000 and R140 000 a month. Then I started to gamble and do tik a lot. I blew R350 000 in six months on gambling and tik. Then things went from bad to worse. Someone told Grace that I was using drugs. I admitted I had a drug problem and she threw me out. I was devastated, I truly loved her.

Six months later I lost my business and all I had left was a bad drug problem.

I met some guys in the drug dens I frequented and we became so called friends. Being a drug addict with no money makes you do stupid things. I had been given some information on a diamond dealer and myself and these guys, who were in the 26s, went to this diamond dealer's house and robbed him at gunpoint, wearing balaclavas.

We left with gold and some diamonds worth about R150 000. We did the job high on tik. I knew the guy also had a safe but did not get to it that evening. I told the one guy that we should go back and get the safe. He told me once you do a job you don't go back.

I said 'Fuck that' and managed to get a police uniform. I returned to the house dressed as a policeman. I arrived at the house at seven the following morning with the man's house keys and watch in hand. I knocked on his door and said good morning, I was sorry to hear about the robbery but that we thought we had caught one of the robbers.

I told him to try the keys in the door but he said he had already changed the locks. So I showed him the watch and he said that yes indeed it was his and invited me in. So we sat down and started chatting about the robbery that had taken place the day before. Because I had information on the guy, I knew he had a gun, so I asked to see his gun licence as it was procedure. I told him that I was not wearing a gun because I hated guns.

He returned with the licence and I asked him to please bring the gun. He returned again and handed me four guns. I ask him whether the robbers had got to the safe and he replied no, that they were dumb criminals, adding that the robbers had asked and he had told them where it was but they left.

I replied that no, they were not that dumb and that they put small cameras in the houses they rob, and then wait for the owner to fill the safe before they came back. I then asked if I could check the house for cameras and also where the safe was.

Once I was in front of the safe, I turned around with the four guns in my hand and told him it was a robbery. After putting him, his wife and son in the toilet, I emptied the safe. I got away with over one million rand in diamonds, R300 000 in gold and R50 000 in cash. I didn't flinch, tik makes you that confident.

I made newspaper headlines the next day. I sold the gold and diamonds for R700 000 and split it with one of the guys from the day before. So I had R325 000, bought a motorbike and checked into a B&B.I gambled and drugged the money out in six weeks.

Then a few months later I got involved with a drug dealer I owed money to, so in return I gave him information about a house that was an easy target. He broke in and stole laptops, jewellery, a television and the car from the garage. Silly me ... I gave him a lift to the house and was caught on camera. I was arrested and was found guilty and got a seven-year suspended sentence.

I was driving a BMW convertible and the car wash guy washed the soft top and fucked it up. The insurance company told me to get the roof replaced, and it was in for repairs at BMW for two weeks. The insurance company gave me a brand new VW POLO with 280 km on the clock to use while my car was being repaired.

When I collected the car at a hire company, they never asked me to sign for the car and being a typical drug addict, thought that there was no proof that I had collected the car. I took the car to a guy I knew who did car repairs and asked him to strip the car for me, he did so and I sold the parts for R50 000, of which I bought drugs and gambled.

I told my sister to drop the key for the POLO at the BMW service department and tell them the car was in the car park. Then I called the car hire company and told them that the POLO key was at the BMW service department and the car was in the car park. A week later they called me and asked where I had parked the car. I said at the car park at the back. They said it was not there and I said sorry, but I couldn't help them.

I went back to the guy who had stripped the car for me to pay him. The police were waiting there to arrest me. I had another car at this guy's place – a two-seater sports car – which he was fixing while also stripping the POLO. So I said to the police that the POLO was not my car but the two-seater sports car was. The policeman then said that the POLO was the car I had hired two weeks previously that had gone missing.

I told the policeman that the guy who stripped the car had gone with me to drop the car at BMW and that he must have stolen the car. I was arrested and was locked up for two nights, my mother got me a lawyer and I got R5 000 bail.

The case got thrown out because BMW said they saw me drop the car off, I got a break in the case. Then they changed their statement and said they did not see me drop the car, it fucked the case up big time. I got lucky.

I met another two guys, also 26s, and we drove around most days buying drugs from various dealers, but one day we had no money so we planned a job. We hit a Gold exchange which was also part jewellery shop. The two guys went into the shop alone at first to sell some gold. They were armed with a tazer gun and a knife, I buzzed the gate and I went into the shop.

One of the men took the tazer and pressed it on the guy's neck. He was alone in the shop at the time and hit the ground with a thud! We all jumped over the counter and dragged the guy to the back of the shop, and tied him up.

I told the 26s not to hurt him. I asked the guy where the keys to the safe were and he said that it was in his car. So I took his keys and he directed me to where his car was parked. I got a laptop and video camera from his car and the keys to the safe. I opened the safe and discovered that it was empty, so I asked this guy why he didn't tell me the safe was empty; he replied 'Would you have believed me?' I had to laugh. There were diamonds and gold medals in his laptop bag. We emptied all the gold and jewels into a cooler box and also took all the cash out of the till.

The next thing a customer rang the bell for the security gate, so I buzzed him in. He had a gold charm bracelet to sell, so I went to the guy who was tied up and asked him for the value of the bracelet, he said R1 000. Then I went back to the front of the shop to tell the guy and then another customer rang the bell, so I buzzed her in, she was a German lady.

I asked her to please wait while I served the other customer. I said to the guy that I could give him R1 000 for the bracelet. He said what does it weigh that I gave him such a price. I weighed it on one of the scales that was on the counter, it was 16.8 grams at R100 per gram it worked out to R1680.

I said to the guy that it was a beautiful bracelet and it was my girlfriend's birthday and that I would buy it for myself at R1 700 and no receipt for tax purposes, he agreed. I paid him and as he left the shop one of my guys panicked and left the shop with him, jumped in our car and had the motor running.

I then turned my attention to the German lady. She asked me where Paul was and I said that he was on the toilet with a bad stomach. She then said the guys outside looked very dodgy. I asked her which guys (thinking she meant my guys in our car), but she pointed to a car outside where the guy who I had just bought the bracelet from was sharing the R1 700 with two other guys in the car.

I opened the front gate and shouted to the guys that they were making this lady feel uneasy. The started their car and drove away. I told my two guys to turn their car off, which they did. I walked back into the shop and the lady asked me why I done that and I told her that I wanted my customers to feel safe in my shop.

I then asked her if I could help her and she said that she wanted to speak to Paul. I shouted to Paul, who was now also gagged, that there was a lady here to see him. I went to the back of the shop and collected all the goods and told Paul to be quiet. I walked back into the front of the shop and told the lady that Paul would be out in five minutes, and that I had to go on an errand. I buzzed myself out, leaving her in the shop, jumped into the car and drove away.

The three of us drove away and booked into a Hotel. The two 26s called a girl to join us. We bought some tik, then called a guy to come and buy the gold and diamonds. We had a big party and then went to the Casino to gamble. We got about R200 000 for this job, two weeks later we were broke again.

Then we decided to rob women of their handbags. I would drive and they would tell me when to stop, they would jump out the car with a plastic gun and rob the women. We robbed about twenty

116

women like that in the space of a month. We would use the cash for petrol and drugs and sell the mobile phones as well.

Then things started to go wrong, we ran out of petrol and we needed drugs. We had R20 and walked to the petrol station and put R20 into a can and returned to the car. In the car were the two 26s, a girl and myself. They told me to stop the car again, after a short journey and they robbed a woman and a young girl. The two women who were being robbed were screaming.

The two 26s in the back of the car had the bag and the girl was sitting in the passenger seat next to me. The next thing we were being chased by security guys in a car, they chased us for a short while and then we ran out of petrol.

So I told the two guys in the back to get out and run and I would take care of the rest, so they did. The security guys shot at them but they escaped, they then turned their guns on me, I put my hands in the air and shout that I was hijacked. The police arrived on the scene and took a two-hour statement from me. They started asking the girl questions but she was in such a state of shock that she could not talk; they told her to return the following day to give her statement. We had no petrol and I told the police that these guys had stolen my wallet and mobile phone, the policeman then gave me R50 for petrol.

I picked up the two guys one hour later and it was a little after midnight. As we were driving home we saw a man who had run out of petrol on the side of the road. They wanted to hijack this guy and I jumped out of the car and said I didn't want to be involved with this. They took my car, hijacked the guy, robbed him, tied him up and left him in a field. They put petrol in the vehicle and stole the car. Now they had their own car and did not need me anymore.

A week later they came to see me, saying they had got someone to fix my faulty starter motor. They left with my car and I did not see them again. I then stole a motorbike and went looking for these two 26s who had stolen my car.

I started to rob women with this stolen motorbike. I would ride past them and it did not matter if their bag was on their left or right shoulder I would snatch it. I would do this twice a day and get mobile phones, cash and cameras, I must have robbed forty women this way.

The police chased me once. I was driving 70 km an hour and hit a wall with my shoulder when I came around a bend. I bounced off the wall and did not feel a thing because I was high on drugs. I rode the bike to a friend who lived nearby and dropped the bike inside his yard. The police followed me to the house and I jumped on the roof and climbed into a neighbour's yard and hid in a dog kennel for two hours until I was sure the police were gone.

I climbed back into my friend's yard and he told me that the women whose bag I had stolen was not going to press charges because she got her bag back. Also they did not confiscate the motorbike because it was never registered, I had stolen a clean bike! I then jumped on the bike and went on to steal another motorbike. I sold the red hot but clean bike to a drug dealer for two grams of tik and R500 cash, it was a R40 000 bike.

So now I am on a new bike and doing my handbag snatching again. I went to a mall and got something to eat, when I returned to the bike the police pounced on me, the owner had spotted me, followed me and called the cops.

I was in jail for one day and got R1 000 bail, I paid it and stole another bike two hours later. I went back to my old ways, and all I wanted to do was feed my drug habit. I then heard that a member of my family had died. I found out later that it was my sister and she had been killed in a car accident. I missed the funeral by about three weeks and although I was sad it was a good thing for me because the police were there to arrest me. If I was there my mother would have died of a heart attack.

I went home after four months of not letting my family know if I was alive or not, arriving on a stolen bike and no car. I was home for three days when the police came and arrested me. In the garage they found the R150 000 stolen motorbike. I was charged with three cases of robbery.

The police told me that the two 26s I used to run with committed fifteen armed robberies, five hijackings and ran away from seven petrol stations without paying in my car. The reason we got caught is because the girl who was with us in the car did not turn up the following day to give a statement and when they went to arrest her she turned state witness.

I spent two years awaiting trial which does not come off my sentence. I believe if I had not been arrested that I would be dead from drugs or have committed more crimes and got a longer sentence.

I was sent to Pollsmoor prison and got attacked by a 28. I was put in a single cell with two other inmates. One of the guys I got to know as Vernon, who was awaiting trial for the rape of nine underage girls and for being in possession of four hundred pornographic images of underage girls.

One evening I awoke and found Vernon hanging from a makeshift rope that he had tied to the top bunk, I jumped up and lifted him up and shouted to the other prisoner in the cell to help me get him down. The other prisoner was awaiting trial for armed robbery and said that I should leave the paedophile to die. I managed to get the rope off his neck and revive him. He recovered and we spoke at length about his life.

I discovered that he was also in a paedophile ring when he was a child; he said that he understood this as love and not lust, and as much I hated what he had done, I could see the good side of this man.

He used to get his sister Elsa to come and visit and my mother used to come and see me. I used to joke with Elsa in the visiting room and we started chatting. I asked if she would like to come visit me and she did. She had a terrible childhood and told me this story about her background.

'I was born in Kuruman on 21st December 1971. Mom divorced my dad when I was still small. He was an arsehole, alcoholic, wife beating paedophile.

I was the second child from my mother's first marriage, my brother Vernon was first. I do not know if she knew my stepdad from before or after her divorce. Fifteen months after me, came brother number two and not long after, stepbrothers three and four were born. Mom's second husband turned out just the same as number one, except she chose to stay with him.

We grew up in a little town called Olifantsfontein in Midrand. At first mom's parents lived with us. Grandpa was a sergeant major in the army. Grandma was suffering from cancer. They were the parents in my life. Grandma passed away in 1978 and I think something of me died with her. Grandpa died a few years later and I was left alone.

We spent a lot of our youth in the Lowveld in a town called Nelspruit, I loved the Lowveld, where we lived on a farm and moved to Gauteng in 1988. I finished school in a town called Boksburg, Vernon went off to do national service, and was stationed in Bloemfontein where he became a jump instructor at the parachute battalion.

I can't say when the abuse started; all I know is that it was always a part of my life. My stepfather would visit my room at night and touch me and penetrate me with his fingers. He wasn't shy I must say. Even when he was sitting in company under a blanket he would be touching me. So I started to refuse to sit on his lap.

Sunday afternoons were rest time and I would be dragged from my room for his little games. So I was a problem child. I have a warrior spirit and I would fight against what I felt wasn't right.

I don't know how he groomed Vernon. It was only once he started having sex with me that he involved my brother. Strangely enough he never touched his own kids though. We have three half-brothers. I was about nine years old when he started having sex with me. Most of the time he would have Vernon and me with him and he would let my brother have sex with me first and then he would. I was a little girl who knew how to give oral amongst other things, charming hey.

Vernon and I went to my mom several times to complain and all she did was chastise us. She caught him a few times and every time I was treated like the villain. That hurt so much. Her betrayal of us is so much worse than the abuse.

Strangely enough all their friends at the time seemed to do the same things. We were abused by the friends as well. So it was a real bugger up. Cause the parents slept with the kids. The children slept around amongst themselves. Very conducive to normal development I must say.

I tried arguing my case with my dad through the years, but to no avail. The argument that it was wrong because he is my dad just felt on deaf ears. He would acknowledge the fact yes, but it was no deterrent. Later you just get into the routine of letting him do his thing or whoever he handed you out to and get up and go on with your life.

At sixteen my mom decided to go back to work and joined the army. Needless to say her in Pretoria and us on the farm in Nelspruit gave him open reign. I called her one day and complained and she said 'Well if it's true go and get help'. Needless to say I did and wasn't loved for it. Vernon was never a fighter so when social services showed up he clammed up. I guess his longing to be accepted was stronger than his desire to get out of the abuse. As for me I was sick of it. Sick of being used and abused, and handed out like a party favour, and most of all sick of my mother's contempt for me. She treated me like a whore and it was her husband that made me into one!

121

I was fostered for a few months and they got me back by convincing social services that I was just lashing out. One of their friend's sons accused his dad when his parents got divorced and they used that as leverage. So I was put back with my abusers and it just picked up where we left off. I guess my track record as a problem child didn't work to my advantage. I was forever fighting and in trouble. I was so bad that I was already working when they were still talking about me at the primary school that I attended. Imagine that infamous!

When I was in standard nine I decided to try and get help again. This time I tried through the church. I remember when the minister came to fetch me they spoke to my parents. My mother's response was 'Did she tell you that he is not the only one?' As if he should have been one anyway! My God!

Of course I was by now also doing my own thing. What did she expect? They taught me from baby years that it was right and just to sleep around, that that is what love is and that is how you measure how much someone loves you. Did they really think that I would be a saint after all they had put me through?

Once again my mom's betrayal totally gutted me. So I was fostered again. I lived with a nice childless couple from the church for a while. Till I took an overdose and back I went to my abusers once again! I finished matric (Grade 12) and I started training as a chef.

Mom killed that dream when she started bitching and moaning about long hours and the little pay I was getting. We had a fight and she chucked me out on the street and I got on the first train back to Nelspruit. I looked for a job that would allow me to finish my training as a chef, but in a right wing racist country at the time I was not allowed to work in a kitchen full of African people. I started nursing at Rob Ferreria hospital. Later I transferred to Kempton Park.

Being that far away from my folks was bliss. I did my own thing, started to gym and lose weight. I had a ball. Then I transferred to Kempton Park and once again I was close to my folks again. And yes the abuse just continued. How does it continue when you are practically an adult? Fucked if I know! I guess when it's all you know, it's hard to break away. I can't answer that even up to today. It just buggers you up so much because now you're an adult and you can't fight this abuse so your anger turns inward as much as outward. You hate them, you hate yourself and you hate God. So yes I was the sunny child in the class!

The abuse continued till two weeks before I got married at twenty-two. So you can imagine the rubbish I took into my marriage. Needless to say we had our issues. My husband knew all these things before we got married but chose to marry me anyway.

I met my husband through mutual friends. I can't say it was love at first sight; today I can't say whether it was love at all. We clicked and four months later we were married, five years later my son was born, this was a blessing and four years later son number two and another two years later son number three was born.

I was pregnant with my last son when I found out the bastard was gay. I stayed with him for another eight years when he was working and not working, I saw his arse through a heart attack and cancer. Then last year he decided to leave because he saw no future with the kids and me, not that he has a future now. He lives with his elderly parents who look after him and he wants half my pension money even though he does not contribute a penny to the boys, Jackass!

Today my relationship with my folks remains a love hate relationship. As long as the distance between us is big enough. They still try to run my life. My dad still tries his luck – what a surprise! So I try to steer clear as much as possible. They hate my kids so screw them. I can't deal with their pre-conceived ideas on rearing children. It's not like they ever won the Mary Poppins award hey. So yes, I am still confused cause I love them and hate them at the same time – will probably be till the day either they or I die.

Where my brother is concerned, I am sad for him. I am also angry at him. Now that he is locked up my folks finally accept him, funny hey. Mom also doesn't want to accept that he is a paedophile, what a surprise! I understand that he only did what he was brought up to do. But I also don't understand because he knows the pain and the damage it did to us. If then we have to go on what studies say, then I am supposed to do the same. Not that I'm the world's greatest mom, Lord knows I fail daily and then some.

Where Bob is concerned, I believe that I'm extremely blessed with him in my life. We have nothing more than what we do right now but it is good. He treats me with respect and always encourages me. I love his sense of humour and his kindness. He is both naughty and nice. Yes we do have challenges but somehow we have this bond.

I know I'm the exact opposite of what he has had all his life but I believe that the quality is better. I am willing to put my heart on the line for him. As long as he doesn't break it. I did not even have this bond with my soon to be ex. His mother is a different story.

I love the old battle axe. She drives me crazy but I love her. Her comments about my weight are uncalled for but I've had that all my life. It's only when she attaches Vernon to her inhibitions that I get upset. Luckily the two of us had that talk and we are okay. We have our roads to travel and we will support each other along the way. I love him and respect him enough to give him a chance. I hope he feels the same.'

As an Author and specifically for an investigative book, I had to keep an open mind and reserve judgement, so when Elsa asked if I would like to visit her paedophile brother in prison where he is serving eighteen years, I agreed.

We arrived at the gates of Drakenstein prison. Known Formerly as Victor Verster Prison, located between Paarl and Franschoek in the Western Cape. I realised that I did not bring my Identity document which has to be presented at two check points before entering the maximum security section of the prison. Elsa told me that she had Vernon's Identity document in her car and I should use it as no one would notice, sure enough I entered the prison with the prisoner's ID that I was visiting through two check points, and he looks nothing like me.

Vernon was nothing like I imagined. Here was a good-looking, charming, polite man and I could not see this man as predator paedophile, but then again how would the Devil come disguised? Not with a scary face and horns on his head, he comes as an Angel.

The question was why would you abuse your own blood if you know how it destroyed and affected your life? The answer was that it was not really full penetration only oral, he only had sex with their friends. He knew that it wasn't right but he was forced to have sex with girls and his sister when he was a young boy and there was something that I relate to love and acceptance.

Vernon did not want to speak about his crimes. Both his daughters are in care and he was sure that they would visit him one day. He spoke about the possibility of moving to another prison where there was a possibility of early parole. We then spoke about his time in the military as a jump instructor at the parachute battalion and it turned out that he was my younger brother's instructor.

Vernon promised to write to me and give me more detail about his life, he never did, and I was not really interested, I could have pulled his court transcripts if I wanted, but did not. I am sure I will never see him again.

Leaving the prison it dawned on me that Vernon was in denial and did not fully accept his crime and perhaps his childhood trauma prevented him from doing so.

Then Elsa asked if I would like to go and meet her parents and I reluctantly agreed. We arrived in the suburb of Bellville and pulled up to a little cottage with a well maintained garden.

Elsa's parents also left me dumbstruck, here was this small-framed woman in her late fifties, with a kind smile who welcomed me into her home and offered me a drink. Her father was a big man who shook my hand and gave me a friendly smile.

Then he asked how Vernon was and demanded that his wife get him a whiskey while he sat on his lazy boy chair watching television. Elsa told me that both her parents have become closer to their son since he was sent to prison.

I looked at Elsa's mother and realised that she was definitely the weaker and was controlled by her husband, but how could you allow your husband to abuse your children, it was beyond me. He was typical middle class management, and her mother was still working for the military, you would never imagine that these two were involved in something so unthinkable, but as I said before, how does the Devil come disguised?

We left and two paedophiles in one day were enough for a lifetime. I asked Elsa why she still visited and respected her parents. Her reply was sad and I felt her pain 'I wanted love and acceptance and as a child that is how they gave it to me, now I feel sorry for them, I forgive them but I will never forget.'

Bob has got a great sense of humour and has accepted the fact that he has to spend at least the next five years in prison. He has become a Christian and was even recently baptized. He has taken up painting and plans to study. Bob says that he and Elsa got engaged when she told him that she would wait for him. She is an amazing person and would do anyone a kind turn. He said they were planning their future together and would start a business again. 'I have made mistakes, I am paying for them.

I am very sorry for the crimes I have committed and especially for all the victims I have left in my wake. I hope they can find it in their hearts to forgive me'.

Damien

The Satanist

Twenty-three-old Damien is a friendly, polite young man, and although he is extremely thin, he has an aura about him that says beware! He has the blackest eyes I have seen and when he stares at you, it feels like he is cutting into your soul.

He told me he could read minds and could judge people in an instant. He also said he trusted me and I was no threat to him. We were sitting next to a field on some crates when I conducted my first interview with him.

At one point he was telling me his story when he stopped abruptly and said there was a snake around, I looked around and assured him that there was no snake – the next thing a snake slithered past us.

There was also a wild cat circling around us and coming very close – wild cats usually run and hide from humans. There was a strange atmosphere and although the sun was shining and it was a hot day, it felt extremely cold. There was a presence here and I felt uneasy, but I prayed to God and immediately felt my Angels surrounding me. I was here to listen to this man's testimony, not to judge him. This is his story.

My mother was eight months pregnant with me when the minister from the local church laid hands on her stomach and prayed in tongues.

I believed that I was touched by God at a young age and that I was blessed. My mother is very religious and she started taking to

Christian cell groups when I was five years old and I had a great interest in the bible.

At home I was a loner and always preferred to rather spend time on my own. I used to watch the other local kids and noticed them playing one minute and fighting the next. I thought that this was what all normal kids did. I started playing with the other kids but I enjoyed hitting them and making them cry. Soon after, they didn't want to play with me anymore.

I continued to spend time on my own and when I turned fourteen I developed an interest in Satanism. I took dogs and would hang them in trees and watch them die.

My life changed and I didn't like anything positive, I did not listen to my mother and my brothers felt like strangers to me.

My father was a 26 when he was younger but now had a job on cargo ships and would spend long spells away from home. When I was a teenager I started hanging around with boys my age, we were all wannabe gangsters but I noticed when any trouble started they would all run away.

I started hanging around with older gangsters who were 26s and 27s. One day I had stolen some Dvds from our house and was walking with my friend Rystam when we bumped into some boys who were in the Bad Boys gang. I asked them where I could sell the Dvds and they asked where I had got them. I said the goods had been shoplifted.

They circled me, pulled out knives, searched me and found my mobile phone that my mother had just bought me. They took my Dvds and mobile phone. I was angry but couldn't fight them because there were too many. Rystam stood one side and did not do a thing. When we walked home I was angry with him for not helping me, I felt like stabbing him.

I then went to school the next day and started to recruit boys for my own gang called the Bone Boys, which meant when we came for you we'd turn you into bones. I wanted revenge.

I was in matric (grade twelve) and now getting into Satanism in a big way. I was holding seances on my own and calling up demons. I drew a pentagram in the centre of my room with candles placed around it, but would cover it with a carpet so my mother would not find out. I studied Satanism online and obtained some books on rituals. I would summon my demon but bind him in my circle and not let him out. I spoke in a language similar to what Christians would call tongues, but this was a negative energy.

I would always perform my rituals at midnight. I started to draw the demons that I saw. I could hear people speaking from a distance, even if they were whispering, my sight improved by 500% and I could read people's minds

There was a demon who followed me around and he would communicate with me telepathically. He had a face like a wolf, his eyes were blood red, his back was like a lion covered in horns, he had shackles and chains on his feet and I could always hear when he was near. At other times he would just float above my ceiling. I wasn't afraid because I was the guardian. Nobody was allowed in my room unless I gave them permission; otherwise the demon would attack them.

One evening my father just walked into my room and the demon attacked him, flinging him all over the room. I got scared and told the demon to leave, I started praying to Jesus Christ and asked for his protection, but now my demon was mad and wanted to kill me.

The clock struck twelve in our kitchen one evening and suddenly I heard my demon running on the roof, I could hear his chains dragging, I then heard a second softer pair of feet. I started to pray again. I ran to my room and put all my sketches in the centre of the room and hid under my blankets. The following morning I went to investigate and found a cat shredded to pieces in our back yard.

I couldn't get rid of my demon. If I thought about him he would materialise. I didn't want to tell my mother and went and asked a Satanist priest how I could bind the demon. This was a mistake because now I got involved in a ritual that would bind me to Satanism even more.

I started getting involved with the coven and we would sacrifice animals and have sexual rituals, which involved having sex while chanting a spell. The ultimate and final point of becoming a Satanist was to drink human blood. I do not know where the blood came from but after we had performed our rituals one evening I was placed naked on a stone slab with a sword while the rest of the coven were chanting around me and praying to Satan. I drank the blood and when I got off the slab I started to levitate, I felt strong but with an extremely negative and evil presence. My eyes turned from green to black in an instant and remain that way up to now.

Now I was ready for revenge and schooled my gang members, the Bone Boys, in Satanism and how to stab people to do maximum damage. We all started smoking tik and on occasion we smoked mandrax to level out. Mandrax is a downer and tik gives you a high and people don't always notice that you are high when on tik. My mother saw that I was out of it when I smoked mandrax, so I just started smoking tik full time.

I was in a field opposite the school one day smoking some tik with another friend called Fifty, he was called this because he was always looking for R50 to buy mandrax. I had long hair and I thought it gave me strength like Samson. A Rasta man walked past us and said that he would tell my parents, I swore at him.

Just then, some boys who were leaders in the school, but not prefects, arrived. They told me to escort them to the head's office. I was the leader of the Bone Boys and had to show no fear. In the passage just before we reached the head's office I pulled out a sharpened pencil and stabbed the biggest boy in the group through the cheek, I was aiming for his eye.

My gang members, who were following behind when they heard I was taken to the head's office, all ran away.

The leaders taking me to the office, I found out later, were members of the Bad Boys gang. They threw me to the ground, pulled out knives and stabbed me in the leg.

There were other gangs in the school, the Dartans, Road Masters, VRMs, KGB, Bad Boys and of course the Bone Boys.

While I was in the head's office and getting suspended for three weeks, some more members of the Bad Boys arrived armed with knives and told a few people that they were going to get me outside the school gates.

The members of the Dartons were watching what was going on and when I walked out the school gates there were about ten of them with chains and baseball bats. They were there to protect me, we approached the Bad boys who were all Britished (ready for battle and armed). They outnumbered us three to one. I told the Dartons that we should wait until the time is right.

I asked the Dartons if they would stand with the number and fight the Bad Boys with me, I said that we must Dala them (kill them).They declined, saying they were peacemakers and only fought when they had to.

I decided then that I would get all the Bad boys who attacked me one by one, the first would be the guy who stabbed me in the leg.

I was with a 26 and we were smoking some tik while waiting for the boy to take his usual route. The 26 said we should also sniff some glue because that would get us worked up and ready for battle. The boy walked past and we chased after him. He was strong and an athlete and easily outran us. He shouted that he was going to bring the Bad Boys to kill us.

I went home later that afternoon and was sitting in the back yard when my younger brother who was thirteen came running in out of breath, shouting that he wanted my machete, close behind him were three Bad Boys.

I asked them why they were attacking my brother if it was me they wanted, and told them to take the battle away from my home.

My friend from the 26s arrived then and asked what was going on, I explained and he said he would go with me. The Bad Boys said they would leave it for this day but now they had a problem with the 26s.

I went back to school after a few weeks and took an axe with me. At break time I saw my friend Fifty run up to me. He was clutching his side and covered in blood. He told me that he had stabbed two members of the Bad Boys several times, but that a third had managed to stab him in the side.

He was arrested and sent to a reformatory, but was lucky not to go to Juvi (Juvenile prison). My mother sat me down and had a heart-to-heart with me, telling me that she knew that I used drugs and that when she looks into my eyes it was not me that she saw but something or someone pure evil.

She convinced me to start going to church with her. I didn't enjoy it at all because it felt like the minister was just doing a job and wanted to just get it over with. My mother tried another church and here things were better. There I studied the bible for a few months and got baptised. I was telling all my friends that I was a pastor – but this would end, when the minister was later arrested for possessing child pornography.

I was disillusioned and decided that the Church was as bad as Satanism and I chose to go back to Satan. I did not go back to the coven but decided to worship by myself. My demon was back and he would tell me to do things. I started dressing in black and would sleep all day and go out at night.

I told people that my new name was Die Duiwel (The Devil) and soon everyone was calling me this. I started to believe that I was the Devil and had to inflict pain, suffering and hate. I did my rituals at midnight every night and spoke to the Devil in Witchcraft tongue. I was now listening to the demon and he was telling me to kill.

I went back to smoking tik and was now stealing where ever I could to feed my habit. I even took my mother's pots and pans to sell for one fix. Sometimes I would rob someone and take all their valuables and if they said just one word in retaliation, I would stab them. I would carry around a big butcher's knife and would stab people at random, even if they accidently bumped into me.

I tracked down some members of the Bad Boys and would watch their movements for weeks. I had been watching one of the boys for some time and one evening I saw him standing on a street corner alone. I walked up to him and stabbed him seven times in the chest, he died on the scene.

This was my first kill and I felt strong and powerful. I was indeed the Devil and would decide who should live and who should die. I licked the blood of the knife and went home to praise Satan. I killed many others after that, there are about six that I can remember, there was more but when I was killing, I blanked out, and only came to when I was licking the blood of the knife.

I also started to take memorabilia, something small, which could be an ear, tongue, nipple, lip, nose, labia, penis and kept it in a jar in my room. When I had just taken a body part, I would offer it to Satan in a ritual and then put it in my mouth so that I could take a part of that person's soul, before placing it into my jar. I never got caught and nobody knew what I was up to.

One day I was at home sitting in my room and my older brother and his friends were having a party in the lounge. I walked to the kitchen and he told me to clean up their mess, he was drunk and showing off. I said I would not and he started swearing at me. He followed me into the kitchen and I pulled out a bread knife and cut the artery in his leg. There was blood everywhere. I ran outside and down the road looking for a victim. But something told me that this was all wrong.

I returned home and was told that my parents were in hospital with my brother and that he had almost died. On their return I hugged my brother – I did not touch anyone unless I was hurting

133

them, I begged his forgiveness and started crying. He said that he forgave me.

My mother told me that I was pure evil and if I did not leave her house that she would kill me herself. I refused to leave and told her if I was going to die, then it would be here in my own room and if it was to be by her hand, then so be it.

I never hurt young people, even when teenage gangsters swore at me or were rude, I ignored them.

I took my revenge against everyone who had ever wronged me – even in the smallest way … sometimes with a knife, other times with a spell.

I am trying to get closer to God, but it is really hard. Temptation is always close and so is my Demon.

Rachel

I wish my sons would die

I got married fairly young and was a nurse at the time. My husband was a policeman. We didn't see each other for days at a time, often working different shifts, and so it went on for a few years.

I gave birth to my first son Johan and eighteen months later my second son Gerhard was born, my daughter Jill was born ten years later. I was very strict with my boys and in their teens when they started going out, I would drop and fetch them.

My husband was a great father to all his kids, and good at his job, he was strict but fair. He became a Warrant Officer and once won policeman of the year but due to job stress, he became depressed – so much so that constantly threatened to kill himself.

It got to the point where he had to stop working, which was worse because now all he did was mope around the house and sink even deeper into depression. He tried to take his life a few times by overdosing on sleeping pills, but I was around to save him every time.

We got him to go for counselling and at first this seemed to work. I was working long hours, often working double shifts to make ends meet and I didn't only have to look after three children, but also a depressive husband.

He was now threatening to kill himself daily and I was considering getting him committed. He spent most days in front of the television smoking sixty cigarettes a day, he didn't help around the house.

One afternoon I had just woken up after sleeping for six hours following a twenty-four-hour shift. I didn't find him in front of the television as usual and went looking for him. I went into the garage and found him hanging from one of the rafters. He must have been there for a while, because his face was blue and his tongue was hanging out. He was still breathing but just barely.

A million thoughts ran through my head. I knew that he was brain-dead and would end up in care, probably my care, for the rest of his life. I could not comprehend or face it. I left him hanging, closed the garage door and called an ambulance. By time they arrived he was pronounced dead.

I think this is where things went wrong with the boys. I never smoked or took drugs ever. When I found out that my boys had a drug problem I stopped drinking alcohol, which I only ever did socially.

I had an outside room at the back of the house and the boys spent a lot of time there. I couldn't always keep an eye on them because I was always working.

I was called from work one day and told that both my sons' had been arrested on charges of possession of narcotics. I was mortified, even though I suspected something, but hoped that I was wrong.

My eldest son was eighteen at the time and would have to appear in court. I pleaded with the police not let them get a criminal record and after a lot of deliberating they were sentenced to fifty hours community service each at the local SPCA.

I think that drugs must run in the family because my husband's family all use some form of drugs. His sister nieces and nephews all use, we never had contact with any of them, so they never knew about my sons' addiction.

My sons' problems got worse and now they were stealing things from the house to sell. I could not leave my wallet on the table for a few minutes or money would disappear.

I sent them off to rehab for six months. On their first weekend back home they were back on drugs.

I had to bail them out a few weeks later because they got caught shoplifting. I sent them off to rehab for a year. When they came out they were great and I got them both a job at the power plant where I was working as a nurse.

I got them the job on my integrity and good name. A few months later there was compulsory drug screening for all workers at the plant. They both tested positive for tik and were suspended, I was mortified.

I sent them off to rehab again for another six months – two months after that stint in rehab they were both on the drugs again.

I had had enough and threw them both out of the house and told them that they could return when they were clean. They slept in their car for a month and once in a while they would call me and tell me that they were hungry. I would go meet them and give them food and watch them eat it – addicts even sell their food for a fix. I would drive away in tears with my heart breaking, but I hoped that tough love would work.

They arrived back at the house a month later and told me that they wanted to clean up and go to rehab. Gerhard has been clean for three years but Johan relapsed after two years.

Johan split from his wife and moved back in with me, but I drug test him on a regular basis and told him that he would be chucked out if I found him positive. I have a teenage daughter and she is my priority and I don't want her around anything negative.

Johan told me his version of events.

I think that it was our father's suicide that was the catalyst in all this. It happened just before my eighteenth birthday and I remember my Mom crying for weeks.

My brother was particularly upset because he had had an argument with my dad on the Thursday and dad killed himself on the Saturday. They never had time to make peace.

I started smoking dagga when I was fifteen, it was more peer pressure from the boys that I use to hang around with. Gerhard always was with me and he too started smoking at the age of thirteen.

We often visited our dad at work and once he arrested a dealer who became my dealer a few years later.

I got a job at a local nightclub when I turned eighteen as a barman where I was introduced to ecstasy. I took a pill before my shift and when I finished I went to the boys I hung out with to score some more. We tried to get some ecstasy but could not get any and a friend said that he could get some tik. I asked what it was and he explained that this was better than any drug ever.

I told him to get us a R100 straw, six of us finished it in about ten minutes. I used the whole weekend, spending R800. By the next weekend my brother was also using. We soon discovered that injecting the tik would give a better high. My mother found out and sent us to rehab.

When we returned my mom got us a job at the power plant where she worked, we were both using and when we were waiting to be tested I asked one of the other guys to give me some of his urine for my brother and I, he told me that he had only smoked dagga. Tik only stays in your system for three days, dagga stays in your system for twenty eight days. The boy lied and the test came back double positive, my brother and I were suspended.

I had a scooter and was driving home one night when the police stopped me for not wearing a crash helmet. They could see that I was high and searched me – they found a lolly and one straw of tik.

I was arrested on the charge of possession again and taken down to the police cells. I didn't want my mother to find out. I was stressed and asked the policeman if I could have a cigarette. He said no, but came back later and handed me a packet. I told him that I wanted to make a statement and would tell them who my dealer was if they did not charge me. The policeman whispered to me that you never say where you get your drugs from and a few hours later I was released.

The next day I went to my dealer and he said to me 'I believe that you were going to grass on me'. I told him that I was going to point out one of the local Nigerians and not him. I knew then that my dealer was connected to the police.

I was still working at the club and when I left one evening I saw two guys standing outside, I asked for a light for my cigarette and noticed that the one guy had a lolly in his hand. I asked him if he had any tik in the pipe and he gave me a few hits. I told them that I didn't have money but we could go sell my mobile phone for more tik. We walked across a field and they pulled out a knife and stole my phone and shoes. They found out at the club that I used tik and I got fired.

I got a job from a man who ran a few shops, and because of my confidence that tik gave me, I was made manager. The owner had no idea. I was skimming money from all the shops and spending it on tik, my brother and I spent up to R50 000 a month on tik. I used so much that I once stayed awake for thirteen days.

I was hallucinating a lot of the time during this spell and was not sure if it was the drugs or lack of sleep. I got out my car and I could not move my arms and I could not walk, I crawled into my car and slept for five hours, when I awoke I told my mother, and was sectioned to a psychiatric hospital in George. I slept for five days.

My brother went to a rehab in Port Elizabeth. After a few weeks he was told that he was not allowed any cigarettes, he packed his bags and hitch hiked to Mosselbay. Before he reached Mosselbay, he had used. He came to visit me in rehab and I could see from his large pupils that he was high.

I was out for a few weeks when I started using with my brother again. My mother found out and she kicked us out the house, she brought us food from time to time, but we were always high.

I went to visit a friend of mine who also used. We were at his parents' house and he had fallen asleep. I was desperate for a fix, so I searched the house and found a box of jewels and went to the local dealer who was also a number.

He said that he could give me only one straw for the jewels but if I returned the next day then he would give me ten more, he took the jewels. I used the tik and returned the following day and asked the dealer for my tik for the jewels. He said: 'Jewels, what jewels?' I couldn't do anything. Dealers often rob their punters and would give you very little for extremely valuable items.

I often left my drivers licence for a R100 straw, because the dealer knew that a new licence would cost me R400.

After a month we decided to go home and ask our mom to help us. When we arrived in the car there were empty syringes all over the dashboard of the car, mom sent us to rehab again

I then met a girl called Sam who was much younger than me. I introduced her to drugs. She preferred cat, but this was not strong enough for me because I could sniff two grams in one go.

We got married and she fell pregnant, six months into her pregnancy she was still smoking dagga and sniffing Cat. We moved to Windhoek, but drugs are easily found anywhere. Our son was born and has a lazy eye. I think it could have something to do with the drugs.

I went to rehab again for six months and when I got out, I got a good job. I did not drink or use anything for eighteen months. I got home from work one day and found my wife smoking dagga with a friend. It went downhill from there.

Tik often gets mixed with heroin so that it is quicker to get addicted and harder to leave because there are physical withdrawal symptoms. Dagga is easy to stop because it is in the mind. I lost my job and my wife could not take it anymore, I told her that I would go and live with my mother for a while and sort myself out.

I am currently clean again and my brother is in rehab. Gerhard told me he had used tik the night before but that this would be last time.

Rachel says she cannot go through it all again. 'Both my sons have been in rehab six times and still they go back to drugs. I have stayed awake many nights wondering if they have been arrested or killed by a drug dealer or overdosed.

I know that they are suffering, I prayed to God to take them, let them die, not because I do not care, but because I love them so much and I am in hell with them every day.

Things have got better for Rachel, Johan has been clean for months, and Gerhard is still in rehab and doing well.

The House

The Defeated, Demented and the Damned

The house is in Oranjezicht, Cape Town. It is an old colonial mansion furnished with antiques and has five bedrooms downstairs and two upstairs, including a storage area and an office.

It started out as a B&B but some guests decided to sign long leases and eventually it ended up as a commune, and new guests would arrive from time to time.

The house is run by Michael, now in his 50s who has lived there all his life, he was brought up there with his sister Mia, brother Deon and his parents. Deon moved away to the suburb of Tableview. Mia was lost to cancer and not long after his mother died, and then his father. The house was put in a trust and jointly owned by Michael and Deon. Michael and Deon promised their father on his deathbed that they would not sell the house.

Michael took out a second bond (mortgage) and turned the family home into a beautiful B&B in 2006. Deon in turn had a change of heart and started putting pressure on Michael to sell, and taking some of the antiques to his new home. The brothers have been at loggerheads since and only communicate through lawyers.

Michael is a staunch Christian but also separates himself from mainstream faith. He is gay and has a preference for young black men. During the renovation of the house a young African labourer named Amos caught Michael's eye.

It wasn't long before Amos moved in and was sharing Michael's bed, even though Michael remained adamant nothing ever happened and they were only friends. Amos can't read or write and was first the handyman and then the house manager. Many guests and house members would complain that Amos was the 'unhandiest' handyman, often taking things apart and not being able to put it together again. Females at the house have also accused Amos of sexual harassment.

After many years Michael and Amos would have screaming matches and flare-ups. Amos started spending more time in his shack in the township.

And Michael frequented gay bars, where he met Marco, a coloured gay man from Namibia, on a night out.

Marco was called 'little madam' by housemates because of his bossiness. Michael was head over heels in love with Marco, twenty years his junior. He played Michael like a harp.

When they met at Crew bar in Green Point, Marco told Michael that he had just arrived in the City from New York where he had had a successful interview with an international airline. He was starting in a months' time and moving to New York. Marco said he was living in a five-star hotel but had some bad luck arriving in the city, having his laptop, money, passport and airline ticket stolen.

Michael started bankrolling Marco on the promise that all the money would be repaid as soon as the insurance paid out. Alarm bells should have sounded when a few days later, Marco told Michael that the thief had managed to cash in his airline ticket and also that he had to pay R600 to have his American express card cancelled.

Michael felt sorry for his new-found friend, who claimed to know no one in Cape Town. Soon Marco was calling Michael skat (precious) and Michael was falling deeper. Marco was spending more time at the house, where Michael was waiting on him hand and foot. Marco was going out every evening until the early hours of the morning and Michael bankrolled his lifestyle.

One afternoon Marco brought home a friend, Lance, who was an Indian man from Durban and had also had some bad luck. Lance was gay and told everyone in the house that he had HIV but it was later discovered that he had full blown Aids and had not been taking his medication. Lance moved in for a few days initially but ended up staying for a few months, all at Michael's expense off course.

Lance was working as a rent boy and his clientele were usually white foreign men. He would stay with his clients for days at a time, often living with them in their hotels. Lance was still going to the dark rooms and hot houses even though he was now rapidly losing weight and spending day's ill in bed.

A club's dark room may be as simple as a small darkened area large enough for three or four people, or may comprise a large portion of the club's floor area, with private nooks, glory holes, (men stick their penises in these holes and would have sex with a stranger or receive or give oral sex) mazes, steel bars resembling prison cells, and varying floor levels.

Some dark rooms incorporate red, black or blue lights – sexual liaisons often take place here. Lance went away with a German client one weekend and on his return announced that he was going into a hospice. Michael got a call from Lance's sister a week later to say Lance had died at home in Durban. The only sad thing about his untimely death was the fact that he knew he had full blown Aids and yet was still sleeping around, whether he used protection only his partners would know.

Marco was visiting family in Namibia at the time and only heard about Lance's death a week later. He came back to the house and was up to his old lies. Michael heard through friends that he never had a top job lined up, had been living in Cape Town for some time and the Hotel he was staying at was in fact the local backpackers. Michael had enough and cut all his ties with Marco.

Keaton, one of the housemates, saw through the whole farce

and wasn't going to keep quiet. He was an old friend of Michael's, gay and also had a preference for dark-skinned men. Keaton had fallen on hard times, and had a tik habit. He was a lecturer at a local college but lost his job through bad attendance.

Keaton initially asked Michael if he could clear a section of the back yard which was overgrown with weeds and pitch his tent. Before he was meant to collect his tent from a previous address, he claimed it had been stolen (later it was discovered that he had sold it to feed his habit).

He asked Michael if he could stay in the adjacent room to his upstairs, for a few days until he could purchase a new tent. Michael decided to let Keaton remain upstairs for a month on a rental agreement.

Michael was losing his patience with Keaton though, because he could hear him clicking his lighter day and night which could only mean he was smoking tik. Keaton brought home an African car guard named Maxwell one evening, and he ended up staying with Keaton for a week.

In that time Keaton accused Michael of having an affair with his boyfriend when he went to work in the mornings. The two had a big argument and Michael threw him out. However a picture taken on Michael's phone was found of a naked Maxwell in his bed. He denied the accusation, saying someone had used his mobile phone and bed.

The room overlooking the backyard was occupied by Siobhan and Johnny, who strongly objected to anyone staying in the back yard as this was an intrusion of their privacy.

Siobhan is the longest housemate, having lived in the house on and off for four years. She is a stylist and worked at top London boutiques in the nineties. She married a French chef, she'd mention to housemates frequently when cooking – but the wine consumed during the cooking sessions took a toll on the taste most of the time.

She returned to South Africa when her mother fell gravely ill, her husband decided to remain in London and ultimately they got divorced.

After selling their apartment in Cape Town there was very little money left over and it was during this time that she found a lump in her breast. She refused to have chemotherapy and instead had the breast removed. She also didn't want an implant. Siobhan, 44 years old at the time, started working at a boutique belonging to a local designer in Long Street.

Long Street in Cape Town has many trendy art galleries, boutiques, pubs, and coffee shops. It is mostly frequented by tourists and students during the day but at night fall becomes a hive of activity, the pubs often spilling out into the streets. Drug dealers and other criminals are often found lurking around and I have often been offered drugs by dealers.

Dealers target tourists and often sell them baby or headache powders, saying it is cocaine. A gangster told me he once sold an unsuspecting customer one gram of 'cocaine' (headache powder) for R400. The customer returned the following evening and complained saying the cocaine wasn't that good. The gangster said he had better stuff but it cost R600 a gram, then sold him the same headache powder, the customer returned twice more to buy the good cocaine (headache powder) at R600 a gram!

Siobhan then met the 'love of her life' as she claimed. Marcus, a local film editor often worked on international projects and met film stars. They met one drunken evening and had slept together – for the first and last time, him saying he loved her as a friend.

Marcus, however, had a serious drinking problem, having spent many stints in rehab without much success. After one six-week stint in rehab at a cost of R30 000, Marcus left the clinic to meet Siobhan in the local pub for a soft drink – the worst place for an ex-alcoholic to go to. He managed to convince her that a few drinks would do no harm, and ended up having several double vodkas neat.

He returned to his parents home a week later, where he was now staying drunk. His parents were absolutely furious and confiscated his car, fearing that he would hurt himself or others. He returned to the house asking Siobhan if he could share her bed for a weekend, saying that he was going to clean up and had a three-month editing job.

The job involved long hours, often starting at six am and finishing six pm, but Marcus decided to work his own hours even if deadlines had to be met. He started his first day (Monday) at nine am finishing at six pm. The second day he started at ten in the morning finishing at five pm. The third day he started at eleven am finishing at three pm. The fourth day he went to work at ten am finishing at midday – and every day he got home drunk. On the fifth day he got fired for breach of contract, which included drinking on duty.

Marcus was now spending his days drinking and sleeping, sometimes not leaving the room for days. Food would sometimes consist of a mouthful of yogurt.

He had a big row with his parents and had not heard from them for some weeks when he got the call that his father had died. His uncle picked him up a few days later to take him to the funeral at ten in the morning – Marcus was so drunk that he had to lean on the car to prevent himself from falling over.

Things got worse when Marcus had an alcoholic seizure one day and the paramedics were called to the house.

He then met up with an old friend Stan and was spending more time with him than with Siobhan, and apparently drinking less. Siobhan was furious because Marcus told her that he and Stan had given each other blow jobs one drunken evening but he was not bi-sexual or gay.

Marcus moved in with Stan but was back at Siobhan's door two weeks later, after Stan wouldn't tolerate his drinking. Once again with no money or a place to live, looking for support from his enabler. This suited Siobhan – as long as she bought him a bottle of

Vodka a day he would stay with her. He managed to stop drinking for an entire week and his appetite returned. He ate like a horse, so Siobhan told him that it would be cheaper for her if he rather started drinking again. Marcus saw this as a blessing.

Marcus was not getting better and Michael was not happy with the situation. After three months Marcus managed to get placed in a rehab for one year and the same weekend Siobhan moved to her own apartment in Sea Point.

This was a blessing in disguise for Johnny, who had been sharing with Siobhan prior to the arrival of Marcus. He now had more room to breathe.

Johnny, who is from a very privileged background and well-educated, realised he was gay at a very young age. He lodged a complaint after one of his teachers hit on him at school. The teacher in question had after many innuendos left a returned exam paper with YES and his phone number written in red ink on Johnny's desk, Johnny returned the paper with a big NO written in black ink. Ironically it turned out the principal was also gay, but never made a move on him.

Johnny finished school and was conscripted into the navy where he became a marine. He enjoyed his navy days more than most other marines and had a fellow soldier who ironed his uniforms in exchange for blow jobs and sex. On completion of his national service Johnny got a job in a top Cape Town real estate company and soon became one of the top salesmen within the group.

He earned good money and was spending a lot of his time in gay bars in town – smoking a bit of dope, using ecstasy, poppers and cat. He had many casual sexual encounters in the dark rooms in the clubs.

The gay scene was at its peak in Cape Town when Johnny was introduced to Frankie through a mutual friend. Although Frankie was ten years his junior, it was love at first sight and that Frankie was bi-sexual didn't matter to Johnny.

149

Johnny bought a penthouse in the trendy area of Moulie Point and Frankie moved in with him. Johnny inherited R3 000 000 from a relative and lavishly decorated the apartment. They now also had more money to party and take drugs. The two also started injecting tik. They were throwing parties for friends and hangers on, often buying the services of hookers and rent boys for themselves and their guests.

Johnny and Frankie frequented a gay massage parlor called Sizzlers in Sea Point at the time.

The house in Sea Point looks like any other suburban house. Walking up the path to the front door, there is a security gate, and behind the gate, a massage parlour for men who are interested in homosexual acts. About 10 masseurs lived in the house together with owner Aubrey Otgaar.

Although it was well-known that Aubrey didn't allow drugs on the premises, most of the prostitutes flouted the rules there.

Two men made a booking for midnight one Sunday evening – a waiter named Adam Roy Woest and Trevor Basil Theys, a taxi operator. Woest worked at a well-known V&A waterfront restaurant which was frequented by Theys and they soon became friends. Adam overheard a conversation that a large amount of money was kept on the premises at Sizzlers and the two of them decided to rob the parlour.

They arrived armed with two pistols, a knife, washing line, duct tape, petrol, balaclavas and surgical gloves, but they didn't wear the balaclavas when entering the property.

Otgaar opened the security gate when they arrived, taking them to a room and enquiring what their preferences were. Woest pulled out a gun and said they were being robbed. The duo took Otgaar at gunpoint to the room where the men slept and ordered the masseurs to hand over their watches, jewellery and mobile phones.

They then ordered the men to remove their shoes and tied their hands and feet and told them to lie face down in a line, they stuffed socks in their mouths and covered it with duct tape. One of the masseurs, Quinten Taylor, refused to lie on his stomach.

Two safes were emptied and then Otgaar and another masseuse were tied together on their request, another masseuse, Sergio de Castro, was discovered in another room with a client named Gregory Berghaus, who also got tied up.

Woest and Theys left the room and returned armed with knives. One they'd brought with them and another they took from the kitchen. They started slitting the men's throats, Woest working from one end and Theys from another. Otgaar managed to break free but they beat, kicked and stabbed him, they eventually severed his carotid artery.

At some point there was a knock on the front door. Theys answered and saw it was a man looking for a masseuse, but turned him away telling the client that they were closed.

They both returned to the room and started sprinkling petrol all over the men; some were still conscious, screaming and pleading not to be killed. They did not set the men alight. This is when Gregory Berghaus managed to break free and started attacking Woest. Theys shot him; Woest then took the gun and shot dead Sergio de Castro.

They returned to the room where the men lay in a row on the floor, Woest started on the right end and Theys on the left, shooting the men in the back of their heads, execution style.

Woest and Theys put on their balaclavas and left the house running to their car parked further down the road.

Quinten Taylor had his throat slit and was shot twice, the first bullet entered his skull next to his left ear, tunneling all the way to his jaw. The second shot entered his head just above the hairline, travelling between his brain and skull into his neck.

Quinten regained consciousness and managed to free his hands and feet, and he ran down the road to a Total petrol station where he collapsed. He survived.

Sizzlers owner Aubrey Otgaar, masseurs Sergio de Castro, Marius Meyer, Travis Reade, Timothy Boyd, Stephanus Fouche, Johan Meyer and Robert Visser, and client Gregory Berghaus, were all killed in the attack. All had been tied up, shot in the head, and had their throats slit.

Woest and Theys were arrested and both gave a full confession to the murders. The received life sentences without the possibility of parole. There is lots of speculation about the reason for the murders, some saying it was a drug debt and others speculating that it was a hit on the parlour through opposition parlours; the truth is that the men confessed to one of the most gruesome massacres in South African history.

Frankie and Johnny never visited parlors after this and just got take aways instead, bringing the men and women when Frankie got the urge, to their apartment.

Both were now injecting tik on a daily basis. They hardly ever left the apartment and would order their food, drugs and prostitutes to be delivered to their home. Johnny had stopped working because he had enough money but two years later all the money was gone and now they were selling anything of value in the house, to the point that they pulled out the kitchen sink and bath and sold this for drugs.

Johnny and Frankie had a few run-ins with the law but it was all drug-related, often ending up in front of the local magistrate.

Frankie was now getting violent when he was not getting his fix and on a few occasions beat Johnny a pulp. Johnny would go and stay with friends for a few days to recuperate and Frankie would follow soon afterwards crying and begging his forgiveness. Johnny always took him back, but things were now out of control and the only thing to sell was the apartment.

One of Johnny's lifelong friends stepped in and contacted Johnny's mother. His parents arrived at the apartment on a day that they were sober and off drugs, but they took one look at the apartment and sent Johnny to rehab for six weeks. Frankie went to

Sasolburg where he managed to get a Job.

It was heartbreaking for both as they had been together for seven years and promised when they were both clean to give it another try. Johnny had spent R3 000 000 on drugs and good times over a period of twenty-four months and all he had to show for it was an addiction. He did however manage to keep the apartment with the help of his friend who renovated and rented it out.

Johnny returned from rehab and lived with his mother for a short spell but then decided that he needed his own space and moved into the house. Michael and Johnny are childhood friends, with Johnny living across the road from Michael for a big part of his childhood.

Johnny wanted to save money and decided to move in with Siobhan whom he had also known for many years. Johnny and Frankie spoke on the phone daily and Frankie announced that he was moving back to Cape Town. Johnny couldn't contain himself because he had not seen Frankie for more than a year. He was counting down the days. The day before he arrived, Frankie called Johnny to tell him that he would not be travelling alone but would be bringing a girlfriend. Johnny was shattered.

Frankie arrived the next day with Liesl who announced that she was pregnant; this was the second blow for Johnny. Frankie then announced that he and Liesl were moving into one of the rooms in the house, blow number three. Frankie and Liesl announced that they were also engaged, blow number four.

Johnny held his head high and would not show anyone the pain that was tearing him up inside. Frankie on the other hand, thought he had scored a double whammy, having both his girlfriend and boyfriend in the same house. He tried his luck but Johnny told him in no uncertain terms that it was now over for good.

Liesl had no idea that Frankie was bi-sexual and even when one of the housemates told her, he convinced her that it was all lies and that Johnny and he were just good friends.

Liesl had a miscarriage and Frankie was distraught. Johnny supported them both throughout this trying time. A few months later Frankie was getting bored with Liesl and was now treating her cruelly, she tried to leave on a few occasions but he cried and told her that she was the love of his life. She also has two young children from a previous marriage but left them with her ex-husband while she was trying to sort out her life.

Frankie stopped her making calls to the kids, saying that he should be number one in her life. Frankie and Liesl left the house and moved to Durban, they were there for a month when Liesl decided to return to her kids. Johnny has left the house and two years later has not used any drugs, he counts himself as one of the lucky ones.

But Michael did not stay single for long; a few months passed and one morning a well-toned African man exited Michael's room. Michael introduced his new friend as Hartley and said that he would be staying for a while as he had fallen on some hard times.

Michael was once again bankrolling Hartley, soon things followed the same pattern and Michael and Hartley would have screaming matches in the early hours of the morning. On many occasions police would arrive, having had complaints from neighbours and housemates alike.

Michael was also physically attacking Hartley if he arrived home in the early hours of the morning, having had his night paid for by Michael.

I visiting the house one day and was introduced to Hartley, who avoided looking at me directly and on another occasion did the same. It then struck me that I knew him. I asked him in front of one of the house mates if he remembered me and he said yes that he knew me from my time I had spent in The Complex with the Hard Livings, he was actually in a relationship with one of the gangster's sisters. I asked him if he was a HL, and he pulled he shirt off and said he had no stamp (tattoo). I told he that he was affiliated, which he also denied.

154

One day a substantial amount of money was taken from Michael's desk. One of the housemates happened to witness the event and told Michael that Hartley had taken it. Hartley went missing for a few days and the police were contacted. On his return late one evening Michael confronted Harley and was screaming and physically attacking him for two hours. The police were called and rather than have Hartley arrested, Michael told the police that they just had a domestic and that he had an order from correctional services for Hartley to live with him at the house.

Harley was in tears and begged Michael for forgiveness. Hartley told Michael that he owed money to the Hard Livings and had to pay them back and that is why he took the money and would pay him back.

Michael forgave him and as usual Hartley got his breakfast in bed the following morning, nothing was said or apologies made to the tenants in his house, as Michael said it was his house and that he could do what he wanted.

Hartley was still in touch with the woman from the Hard Livings and she managed to get hold of Michael's mobile number, she told him that Hartley also owed her money and wanted to know what his and Hartley's relationship was. Michael told her that he was just helping him as a friend. One evening Michael received a call from one of the Hard Livings who told Michael that he was going to bring some boys around to the house and that he would rape Hartley and himself. After hearing this I decided to stay away from the house because I knew trouble was brewing.

One evening there was another turn of events, I was told this story by one of the housemates.

Hartley arrived home late one evening and Michael was having a braai (barbeque) with some housemates and some of their friends. Michael followed Hartley to their bedroom and a shouting matched ensued. Michael called for help and one housemate and two of his friends ran to the bedroom where Hartley was standing partially dressed.

The two men who followed the housemate were known x-special forces and one was presently on bail for murder. Michael told the men that Harley was hitting him and one of the men struck Hartley to the ground with one blow. The two Special Forces men then carried him to the coach where they continued to assault him. They asked Michael what they must do and Michael replied get rid of him, meaning of course throw him out the house.

The men took it literally. One of them asked for cable ties and said that they would remove the body when everyone had left. Hartley was crying hysterically and pleaded for his life. Michael did not intervene or was afraid to.

One of the men told Hartley to put on his best clothes so that he could go out in a dignified manner, he would not feel the bullet enter the back of his head he was told. The housemate present pleaded with the two men and they left and joined the party.

Harley slept very badly that night, but the following morning all was forgotten and Hartley got his breakfast in bed as usual. I think the house is heading for disaster and nobody knows when, but all know it is coming.

The House seems to attract the defeated, demented and the damned.

Oliver

Cruelty

I met Oliver at Elpetra Ministries. He was feeling under the weather on the Wednesday he spoke to me. The twenty-six-year-old is a well-spoken educated young man. This is his story.

I was born in Belgravia on the Cape flats. My father has two sons from a previous marriage. He has a psychology de-gree but works in sales and marketing. My mother is a senior prosecutor.

I spent most of my childhood with my grandparents, I use to call them ma and pa. Pa started to masturbate in front of me one day when I was four, and when he ejaculated I asked him what it was – he said that it was milk.

One evening after I got home I asked my mom when I would have milk? She asked me what I meant and I told her how pa had played with his winkie and milk came out. My mother called the police and pa was charged, locked up, bailed and had to appear in court the following month.

Ma told pa that she was leaving him and the day before pa was to appear in court he killed himself. Ma didn't let me visit with her anymore and when I did, she told me that it was my fault pa was dead.

My parents divorced and my father remarried what I call the stepmother from hell. I nicknamed her Cruela. My brothers and I shared a room. At five I was the youngest, my stepbrothers were only one and two years older than me. We were not to leave the room after lights out at eight at night and had to use a potty if we needed the toilet.

We were all in bed one evening and I was scared to get up in the dark to use the potty and wet the bed. The following morning my stepmother came into the room and saw had happened. She told me to stand next to my bed and picked up the full potty and poured it over my head. I told my mother on my next visit to her and she approached Cruela who told her that I was exaggerating and that she accidently spilled a bit of urine on me when she picked up the potty. Now Cruela really had it in for me.

I started living with my mom but had to spend every other weekend with my dad and Cruela. When we were in the room she told me that if I sat on the bed my feet were not to touch the ground, because the Devil was watching and would pull me down to hell where I would burn forever.

When I was six years old we went on holiday to Montague Gardens. On our way there I was sitting in the back of the car with Cruela's two sons, I was wearing shorts and she turned around and pinched my leg. I said nothing. She smiled and asked if it was sore and I said no, just loud enough so that my dad, who was driving, could not hear. She pinched harder and asked again if it was sore, I said no because I wasn't going to give in to her. She did it again, this time drawing blood, and now and although my lip was quivering and I had a tear in my eye, I just shook my head. She just grinned.

I was up early in the morning on the first day of our holiday, I was so excited and could not wait to explore. I found Cruela in the kitchen washing dishes with sunlight liquid soap in one sink and dish towels soaking in Jik (stain remover) in the other sink. I asked Cruela if I could get some Wheetbix cereal because I was only six and could not reach the shelves. She handed me a bowel with two Wheetbix and filled with milk.

It smelled like a mixture of soap and Jik and I told Cruela that it tasted funny. She told me to shut up and eat all my breakfast and that I was not to leave the table until I had finished. With each mouthful I almost wretched and started crying and told her I could not eat it.

She said that I had to eat it if I wanted to go out that day. I forced myself to eat it, I wanted to go out and have a nice holiday. When I left the table I ran to the toilet and vomited. I was feeling very ill and I got a runny stomach. Cruela told my dad that I had better stay in bed for the day and that's where I stayed for the next week.

On the last day of our holiday I was finally feeling better. My dad said that we would all go to the beach for the day, but Cruela convinced him that we should rather stay in because they had all been out every day. She looked over at my disappointment and grinned, I understood what hate meant that day. I never told my Dad about any of her cruelty.

I was a very polite child and respected my elders, but whatever I tried or did, Cruela always was cruel.

I started getting into fights at school and found that it was easier to earn people's respect this way. I was now fourteen and no longer going to my dad's for weekends.

I was spending time with my older cousin who gave me heroin to smoke one day, and I was so ill that I didn't take any drugs again until I was sixteen. I met a group of friends and started smoking dagga until I was eighteen.

I met a beautiful girl from Scotland and fell in love with her, she had a cocaine habit and soon I had one too. My older cousin was also back on the scene and introduced us to crack cocaine and heroin mixed. Crack is the upper and heroin is the downer, so you were always just level. I also started experimenting with other drugs now.

My girlfriend was getting out of control, wanting more of a high and so started injecting heroin. I always only smoked it. She overdosed on a few occasions but we always got her to hospital on time, until we both fell asleep after she'd injected one day. When I woke up some hours later she wasn't breathing. I called an ambulance but when the paramedics arrived they said that she had been dead for several hours. Her death devastated me, I decided to clean up and quit drugs for good.

I got a job with Mango airlines as a steward when I turned nineteen. I loved it. I bought a nice car and clothes and had a few girlfriends but was non-committal. I bought a second car.

When my cousin just got out of jail we went for celebratory drinks. I was loaded and later that evening we ordered some rocks. It was the beginning of another downward spiral.

I was told to take a random drug test at work – I had heroin and morphine in my system and was forced to resign, the company had a zero drug tolerance policy. One of the girls who worked with me also got dismissed that day because of drugs and we went back to her flat and smoked tik for the next three days.

I took heroin to come down but then also became very depressed. I had one of my cars parked in my granny's garage and took two hose pipes, sealed them onto my exhaust and put them in my window, I switched on the car and started feeling drowsy, I panicked but couldn't move. I didn't want to do it but knew it was too late. I heard the window being smashed. My granny had heard the car and was checking if it was me and in doing so saved my life.

I cried and told her that I lost my job and that I was sorry that I was responsible for pa killing himself. She told me that she loved me very much and that she had only said it in a moment of anger but never meant it. It was like a weight had lifted off my shoulders by something that had been said in a moment of anger almost sixteen years ago. This was a lesson on how words can create joy or pain in someone's life, and most of the time we aren't even aware of it.

I told my mother that I had a drug problem and was amazed at how calmly she took it, she asked if I was still using and I said no. I lied. I started using tik full time, because you can still function when you are using tik and you feel that you are totally in control.

My friend Jonas was at college doing business studies and we

160

decided to start a clothing business together. Whenever I was high I would work on this project, which was every day for one month. I drew up a business plan and even had potential investors.

My friend was very impressed and to my disappointment, I later discovered that this was a task that was part of his course. We haven't spoken since.

The other problem with drugs is when you are high, you have the greatest ideas but the next day all you want is the next fix. Now I was running short of money and started stealing from home.

I still had two cars and sold one for R100 000 so that I could make monthly payments on the newer model. I was dipping into my car fund for tik, three months later my bank balance was R16.25. I started using crack and heroin again; soon I was selling everything I had of value. I stole all my mother and grandmother's jewellery for drug money.

I walked into the dealer's place one day and had designer gear on from head to toe. My merchant had a girlfriend Ju Ju, who also worked as a prostitute, and she asked if I wanted to sell some of my clothes. I sold my Adidas top, Diesel jeans and Nike trainers for three bags of tik. I walked out in my underpants.

I asked my mother for help and told her that I had a serious drug problem. She sent me to a five-star rehab for three weeks at a cost of R30 000. I tried to smuggle drugs into the rehab and lost all my privileges after one week.

I was diagnosed with ADHD and OCD while in rehab. I sold all my personal belongings in rehab so that I could have drug money when I got out. The first day out of rehab I smoked crack.

My friend Jonas's girlfriend was pregnant and when she had the baby, he wanted nothing more to do with her. I went to visit her and the new baby one evening. I told Jonas that I had been to visit Natasha, he went berserk and attacked me. We ended up beating each other up so badly that I had to go to a doctor to get pain killers and sleeping pills.

I took some pain killers and two sleeping pills and while half asleep I took another eight. My parents found me unconscious with the almost empty bottle of sleeping pills next to my bed. My father went crazy and started beating me with his fist. I have never heard my father swear or seen him so angry. I was sure he would kill me. I called to my granny for help. The following day my mother threw me out the house.

I had nowhere to go and decided to pick up Natasha from work. Natasha had a spare room in her flat and said that I could stay. Jonas was even more upset. I thought: this is payback for the clothing deal you pulled. I told Natasha that evening that if I had met her first, then she would have been my girl. She said that she had always liked me, one thing led to another and we ended up in her bed together.

We decided to start a relationship and after four days I left drugs, Natasha never used. One month later Natasha got retrenched. We had no money and I started shoplifting small items ... . belts, shoes and underwear.

Then I got smart. We would go shopping at Woolworths, which had an exchange policy even if you do not have a receipt. I would walk into the store and fill my trolley with towels duvets, anything and take it to the refund counter.

I would go to different Woolworths stores and make an average of R5 000 a day. One day Natasha was with me and we had refunded goods for R10 450 at a store. My mistake was when I left with the exchange vouchers in hand, I took a trolley and filled it with blankets and towels and walked out the store. I got locked up at the local police station for forty-eight hours; I went to court and was in the court holding cells which was a frightening experience.

There were beatings and robberies of Franse by the numbers here, a ferocious man who was a number 26 came up to me and asked where my money was, I told him I had nothing on me. He went to the man next to me and started going through his pockets, just then a warden arrived and saw what he was doing and started beating this number with his truncheon.

He was gone five minutes then the robbing and intimidation went on. I got a nine month suspended sentence for two years. I could work this scam for a while but my car payments were three months in arrears. I had to find a new scam.

I know moved up the ranks of crime and into fraud. My friend was making good money and I wanted in. We call it the Jockey scheme.

You find someone who is desperate for money, and there are many of those. You make a payment of R15 000 into the Jockey's account and mark it salary. Then we get a company (and there are many of those) to issue a pay slip and confirmation of employment.

We then would get a one month statement and one can get a loan with the African Bank. We would then take out a personal loan for R36 000 in four micro loans of R9 000 each. The handler or Jockey gets half and we take half. Then we'd get credit for furniture for R39 000, we'd sell the furniture for R19 000 and give the Jockey R5 000. We then pay the loan for three months so that we get more credit.

We took delivery of two cars from one Jockey, one was a BMW32I and the other was a brand new Mazda. The Mazda was with Wesbank. We had a connection there, a woman whose brother had a business and we bought the car through his business without him knowing. The following day the car dealer phoned the brother to congratulate him on his new car.

He phoned his sister at the bank and she told him that there was some mistake and that she'd sort it out. She called us and we took the car and left it in front of the dealers with the keys in the ignition. This was too close for comfort and we decided to stop the scam for a while. We had R70 000 in cash from our scheme and the temptation was too much for my friend – he ran away with all the money.

I had to go back to shoplifting, and all the money I got went on tik. I went to Pick & Pay and shoplifted two DVD players, then sold them and bought some tik. Two hours later I went back to the same Pick & Pay and stole another two DVD players – this time I was caught. I still had a suspended sentence and was sure that I would go to prison.

But I was sent by court order to rehab for twelve months. I will change my ways, because my girlfriend is three months pregnant, but I don't know what to do when I get out.

I heard later that Oliver had run away from rehab and was caught shoplifting soon afterwards. He is currently serving a two-year sentence at Pollsmoor prison.

Dewani

Murdered

Anni Dewani was found dead inside the back of a vehicle on the morning of 14 November 2010 at 07:50. She had been abducted the previous evening, and had suffered a single gunshot wound to her neck. What followed next would make international headlines and her husband, Shrien Dewani, would become the prime suspect in her planned abduction and subsequent murder on their honeymoon.

Anni Dewani (nee Hindocha) was a Swedish-born ethnic Lohana Hindu. The Hindocha family lived in Uganda and was forced to leave the country in the early 1970s after ruler, Idi Amin, expelled all Asians living there. They were granted residence in Sweden, where their daughter, Anni, was born and raised.

After training as an engineer, she joined Ericsson. Shrien Dewani, also a Lohana Hindu, was born in Bristol, England, and raised at the family home in Westbury-on-Trym. He was educated at Bristol Grammar School and then the University of Manchester Institute of Science and Technology, where he qualified as a chartered accountant with Deloitte Touche Tohmatsu Limited, commonly referred to as Deloitte, working in the City of London. In 2005, he resigned from his position to help found and run his family's chain of PSP Healthcare old age homes.

Anni met Shrien through mutual friends while visiting her cousin, Sneha, in Luton, Bedfordshire, England in 2009. Shrien proposed to Anni at the Ritz Hotel, Paris, in June 2010, with a twenty-five thousand pound diamond engagement ring balanced on a red rose.

The couple married in Mumbai, India, on 29 October 2010; 500 guests attended the traditional three-day Hindu ceremony. The couple decided to honeymoon in South Africa.

After landing at Cape Town International Airport, the couple took a domestic flight on 7 November 2010 to the Kruger National Park game reserve where they stayed for four nights. The couple returned to Cape Town on 12 November. Shrien approached Zola Robert Tonga, who operates a shuttle, at the airport and he drove them to their hotel in his VW Sharan.

On arrival at their hotel, and while Anni Dewani was checking in, Shrien had a seventeen-minute conversation with Zola in the front of the hotel – allegedly to procure a hit man.

On the evening of 13 November 2010, Anni and Shrien arranged to be driven by Zolo Tongo to a restaurant in Strand, where they had dinner overlooking the Atlantic. After dinner, the couple went for a walk on the beach. Anni apparently said she wanted to see the real South Africa and Zolo suggested visiting Mzoli's in the township of Gugulethu.

Mzoli's is named after the founder and owner, Mzoli Ngcawuzele. It is also known as Mzoli's Palace and is popular amongst locals and tourists. When entering Mzoli's, your first stop is at the butchery, where you choose your meat and the sauce you want it cooked in. You then hand it to the BBQ section, where a number of employees barbeque your meat to taste.

Mzoli's doesn't have a liquor licence and it is advisable to take your own, but there are local shebeens in the immediate area where you can obtain alcohol at a reasonable cost. The word shebeen derives from the Irish word Sibin, meaning 'illicit whisky'.

Next door to the butchery is a big hall with tables with seating for up to three hundred, with an adjoining dance floor; African music blares through speakers with a local or national DJ. The people here are extremely friendly and make you feel very welcome.

Anni and Shrien never got to see Mzoli's.

What happened next would make world headlines.

Mondo Mbolombo

Zola Tonga approached Mondo Mbolombo at the Colosseum Protea Hotel in Century City, where he worked as a front desk clerk, on 12 November 2013. Mondo was an acquaintance of his and Zola asked to have a private conversation.

Zola asked Mbolombo if he knew anyone who was a hit man. Mblombo said he did not, but that he would contact an old friend known as 'Abongile' or 'Spra', who turned out to be Mziwamadoda Qwabe. Mondo used his mobile phone and his employer's phone to facilitate the process.

On 13 November, Mbolombo met Qwabe at Monwabisi beach, where he asked him for a bullet, because he wanted to perform a traditional ritual.

They parted ways and, later that day, Mbolombo received a call from Qwabe, who said that he was looking for Zola, who had arranged to meet with him. Qwabe also told him that there was a lady who needed to be killed, and that the gentlemen who wanted the lady killed was not from South Africa – it was to be staged to look like a hijacking.

Qwabe, Zola and Mbolombo were in constant telephonic contact from approximately three in the afternoon till eleven that night.

Mondo Mbolombo would later be offered indemnity from prosecution if he told the truth – but the court eventually found him to not be a credible witness.

Mziwamadoda Qwabe

Mziwamadoda Qwabe (also known as 'Abongile' or 'Spra') was a friend of Xolile Mngeni's and had known him for approximately eight to nine years; Xolile lived about a five-minute walk from him. On 12 November 2010, he received a call from Mbolombo, who told him: 'There is a job that needs to be done'.

Mbolombo told Qwabe that he would give Qwabe's number to Zola Tonga. He received a call at about seven that evening from Zola. Xolile Mngeni was with Qwabe at the time and Qwabe referred to him as Watti. Zola Tongo told Qwabe that there was a husband who wanted his wife killed. Zola asked Qwabe how much it would cost to do this, whereupon Qwabe conferred with Xolile, who suggested an amount of R15 000. Then they made arrangements to meet the following day so they could discuss what had to be done.

The following day, Saturday, 13 November 2010, Zola called and arranged that they meet in Khayelitsha. Zola and Qwabe met at a place called Khaya Bazaar. Qwabe called Xolile and asked him where he was, and Xolile said that he was out at his friend Lukhaya's house in Sidima Circle, Khayelitsha. Zola and Qwabe then drove there to meet with Xolile. They parked outside Xolile's friend's house.

Xolile came out and got into the back of the vehicle. Zola then told Qwabe and Xolile that there was a husband who wanted his wife killed. It had to look like she'd been killed during a hijacking. The assassination had to take place near Mzoli's Tavern in Gugulethu.

Zola also told Qwabe and Xolile which route to take and where to meet him. It was agreed that Zola would leave the R15 000 in the cubbyhole of the vehicle. There was no specific instruction on how Anni Dewani was to be killed. Zola Tongo's phone would also be taken during the hijacking. At eight that evening, Zola called Qwabe and said that he was on his way to Gugulethu. Qwabe and Xolile were on their way to Gugulethu when Zola called and cancelled.

Qwabe and Xolile went back to Khayelitsha and went their separate ways. Later that evening, between ten and eleven, Qwabe received a call from Zola to say that they were on their way from Somerset West to Gugulethu. Qwabe went to an acquaintance of Xolile's, Mwanda Vanda, where Xolile was. Qwabe arranged transport with Mwanda Vanda to go back to Gugulethu. Qwabe then drove Mwanda's vehicle to Gugulethu until they reached the area of NY112. Qwabe and Xolile got out the vehicle and agreed to meet on the corner of NY112 and NY108.

Qwabe received a text message from Zola to say that he was close by. Qwabe was busy urinating when Zola's vehicle approached. Xolile stopped the vehicle and pointed a firearm at Zola. Xolile instructed Zola to get into the back seat of the vehicle. Qwabe got behind the wheel and drove. He stopped the vehicle on the corner of NY1 and NY111, and ordered Zola to get out. Zola's phone was taken from him before he got out the vehicle. Zola whispered to Qwabe that the money was behind the front passenger seat.

Qwabe drove to Khayelitsha near an informal settlement at Kuyasa and ordered Shrien Dewani to get out the vehicle and go to one of the houses nearby. While Qwabe was driving between the areas of LLitha Park and Ndlovini, he heard a gunshot go off in the vehicle.

Qwabe and Xolile drove to LLitha Park and parked the car on the pavement. Xolile was looking for the cartridge; Qwabe assisted him and found the cartridge on the mat in the back of the vehicle. Qwabe threw the cartridge into a drain. Qwabe and Xolile then both walked away.

Later, when they counted the money, they found that there was only R10 000 and not the agreed R15 000. Xolile also had R4 000 in cash, which he had taken out of Shrien Dewani's pocket. Qwabe and Xolile shared the money. Xolile also had three mobile phones and a digital camera. The following day, which was 14 November 2010, Xolile brought the firearm back to Qwabe, as it belonged to him.

Qwabe was arrested later that week and agreed to co-operate with the police. He had the opportunity to speak to Xolile, who told him that he had told the police the truth. Qwabe made a full confession to the police on 18 November 2010. Qwabe, however, became very bitter when he found out that Xolile had pointed him out as the person who had shot Anni Dewani.

Qwabe said in his statement that he agreed with Xolile that he would do the driving. Qwabe denied pointing the firearm at Zola and shooting Anni Dewani. Qwabe said that he could not recall at which point he handed over his firearm to Xolile.

There were twenty-six witnesses in the murder trial of Anni Dewani. Here are a few of them.

Daisy Mpongwana

Daisy Mpongwana, who is an elderly person, said that she was in the area of Sidima Circle at approximately 15:30 on Saturday, 13 November 2010, when she saw Xolile and Zola sitting in a car. Both were known to her. She was glad to see Zola, who used to stay near her. She had recently moved to the area where Xolile stayed.

Sipho Qakaza

Sipho Qakaza confirmed Mrs Mpongwana's statement that on Saturday, 13 November 2010, at midday, he saw Xolile and Qwabe sitting in a vehicle in Sidima Circle. He also stated that he had seen Xolile and Qwabe on a regular basis in each other's company.

Xolile told Sipho that he would meet him at Lukhaya's house. Xolile met Sipho at Lukhaya's house, where Xolile arrived with a plastic bag. He took out a gun from the bag, which was later identified as the gun used in the killing of Anni Dewani. The following day at approximately midday, Sipho saw Xolile speaking to a neighbour, and he joined them. He saw that Xolile had a Prada watch in his hand. Sipho asked if he could have the watch. Xolile refused and left.

Xolile returned a bit later with a ladies' Georgio Armani watch which he wanted to sell for R400. Xolile returned to his shack, while Sipho waited for him. When Xolile returned, he was wearing a pair of Lacoste takkies. Xolile then took out a camera, a Blackberry and a Nokia. Sipho took the camera and switched it on, and on it Sipho saw a married couple in one of the images. The man was wearing a suit and the woman was wearing wedding clothes. Xolile asked Sipho to delete the images. Sipho later saw on television that the woman in the picture was the tourist who had been killed.

Lukhaya Bacela
Lukhaya Bacela and Xolile Mngeni were childhood friends. Xolile arrived at Lukhaya's house in the early hours of the morning on 14 November 2010. Xolile told Lukhaya that he had picked up a Nokia Phone in Llitha Park. Later that Sunday, they went to the V&A Waterfront, where Xolile bought Lacoste takkies and a jacket. They went their separate ways and, later that day at five, they met again and this is when Xolile told him that he had robbed and shot a woman in Llitha Park. Lukhaya was arrested with Xolile in the early hours of the morning on 16 November 2010. The police found a Nokia under the mattress where Xolile was sleeping. Bacela's aunt later told the police that she had found other items of jewellery in the shack.

The Police
The Dewani case was led by investigating Officer Captain Paul Hendrikse, from the Hawks. One of the first policemen to arrive on the crime scene was fingerprint expert, Warrant Officer Hanekom, from the South African Police Services.

The VW Sharan was taken to the SAPS vehicle storage unit in Stikland where fingerprints were taken from the vehicle. A left palm print was lifted from the right fender and bonnet of the vehicle. It was scanned into the SAPS Automatic Fingerprint Identification System (AFIS) – a database held by the SAPS of people who have had brushes with the law.

It was found that the left palm print belonged to Xolile Mngeni. On 14 November, Captain Clifford Smith retrieved a bullet from the VW Sharan, from the back cushion of the right back seat.

On 18 November, a firearm was recovered by Colonel Theron of the SAPS. This was sealed and handed to Captain Paul Hendrickse and then to Captain Clifford Smith of the SAPS Provincial Crime Scene Investigations. A cartridge was retrieved from a drain at Singolamti Street, Llitha Park, Khayelitsha, on 19 November 2010, which was pointed out to Warrant Officer Van Der Berg by Mziwamadoda Qwabe. It was sealed and handed to the SAPS ballistics unit.

Captain Paul Hendrikse recovered a Nokia mobile telephone that belonged to Zola Tonga on 16 November 2010 at C394 Sidima Circle. Also recovered from C394 Sidima Circle were an Armani ladies' wrist watch and a silver bracelet, which was found by Alice Mcinga. The Blackberry 9700 was recovered from Phumezo Nzotho after Xolile had sold it to her for R500.

Warrant Officer Engelbrecht examined the fired bullet that Captain Clifford Smith found, the cartridge that Qwabe pointed out and the 7,62mm Norinco pistol. He provided the location of the person who had shot the deceased and the distribution of gunpowder residue after the shot was fired. In his expert opinion, he also stated that the weapon could be prepared and fired with a single hand.

The following items were taken from the Dewanis during the hijacking: Georgio Armani wrist watch; white-gold diamond bracelet; ladies' handbag; Blackberry mobile phone – estimated value R90 000. All these items were used as court exhibits, including firearm, ammunition, CD and a police video pointing out the scene of the crime.

Dr Jeanette Verster conducted the post-mortem examination and found that Anni Dewani had died as a result of a single gunshot wound to the neck. The bullet travelled through her hand and into her neck. She was shot at close range and the barrel of the weapon was five to ten centimetres from her when the shot was fired. She also concluded that Anni was in a defensive position when the shot was fired and the gunshot tract was consistent with a single shot.

Xolile Wellington Mngeni
Xolile is twenty-five years old, unmarried and has no children. His highest standard of education is Grade Seven. He was diagnosed with an unusual malignant tumour, which originated from the pineal gland situated within the brain. In May 2011. Xolile underwent surgery and had 70% of the tumour removed. The tumour had completely disappeared according to a MRI scan in May 2012. Dr Parkes, an oncologist and head of the Clinical Unit of the Department of Radiation Oncology at Groote Schuur, Cape Town, was of the opinion that there was a fairly high chance that the tumour would reappear. She also stated that survival rate for a person suffering from this condition was between two to five years.

After his arrest, Xolile lied about his involvement in the murder of Anni Dewani. He said that he was not with Qwabe on 12 November 2010 when Qwabe received a call from Mbolombo. Xolile said he was going to a shop, which is opposite Bacela's house, when he met Qwabe, who was sitting in a vehicle. Xolile said that Qwabe had asked him if he knew anyone who would want to buy a phone. Xolile said he would let him know the following day. When he saw Qwabe the next day, he had two mobile phones with him, a Nokia and a Blackberry.

Xolile said that on Sunday, 14 November 2010, he was on his way from his girlfriend when he met Bacela. They went and bought takkies (trainers) and a jacket at the Waterfront. Xolile said Bacela was lying and he had not gone to Bacela's shack in the early hours of the morning. He said Bacela was lying when he said that he had robbed and shot a woman.

Xolile said Vanda was lying when he said that he was in the car. He said the reason Vanda lied was because he had a fight with his brother in 1999 or 2000. Xolile said that Qakasa was lying when he said he had seen Xolile with two watches and a camera in his possession. Xolile said he was not in a position to use a firearm because he had had an operation on his elbow and lower arm.

The court found that the state's case against Xolile was beyond reasonable doubt. The evidence against Xolile Mngeni was overwhelming. The common purpose was the murder of Anni Dewani for a payment of R15 000 to be shared by Xolile and Qwabe. Anni Dewani was murdered, and robbed after she was dead.

The South African court was very harsh in its condemnation when it dealt with contract killings such as the present.

In KGAFELA 2001 (2) SACR 207 (B) at para 81-85 where Friedman JP held that:

"(81) Society has not, and will not and cannot tolerate murder attendant on an 'assassination contract'. This has been designated as a heinous crime by our courts, which inspires a sense of revulsion and horror, and strikes at the root of social order. To consider that gratuitously, or for payment, a person may be hired to take the life of another is a chilling thought, whatever the circumstance.

(82) Our courts have a whole series of judgments visited on hired killers and persons who acted in concert with them with severe punishment. See Mlumbi en Ander 1991 (1) SACR 235 (A) S v Dlomo and others 1991 (2) SACR 473 (A).

(83) Assassination contracts contain profound dangers and are a type of atrocity to be combated, and the courts duly, in the discharge of its function, visit such perpetrators with the severest punishment. As MT Steyn JA once stated, this type of crime exemplifies and gives sombre meaning to the expression 'homo homini lupis' (man is a wolf to man).

(84) In consequence of the foregoing, the hiring of assassins has been treated as a serious aggravating factor. When a person is convicted of murder by hiring a killer, the court, in considering sentence, takes into account the well-established triad, namely: 1.

The offender as a person; 2. The nature of the crime and the manner in which it was committed; 3. The interest of the community affected thereby. The courts also take into account the purposes of punishment, namely, deterrence, prevention, reformation (rehabilitation) and retribution. The objectives of deterrence and retribution emerge in the forefront of the process in the punishment for the crime of assassination.

(85) It must be so, as this is a method of expressing the instinctive public reaction and the perception of this horrendous crime.

Xolile was charged with robbery with aggravating circumstances and the premeditated murder of Anni Dewani, contravening Section Three of the Firearms Control Act 60 of 2000 in that he was in possession of a firearm without being the holder of a licence or permit to possess such a firearm.

This was also in contravention of Section 90 of the Firearms Control Act 60 of 2000: the unlawful possession of ammunition without being the lawful owner of a firearm from which such ammunition can be discharged. He was acquitted on the charge of kidnapping.

When I went to visit another prisoner whom I was interviewing at Brandvlei Correctional Services, and whom I formerly knew from Scotland, I was given an introduction to Xolile. I made arrangements to visit him.

Xolile arrived in the visiting area at Brandvlei Correctional Services Maximum in a walking frame. He was very unsteady and his speech was slightly slurred due to the medication he was taking.

His English wasn't very good but we managed to communicate, we made some small talk and then he proceeded to tell me that he had had a number of operations to remove his brain tumour.

He said that he believed that the tumour was due to the beating he endured at the hands of the SAPS. He stated that the police had tried to suffocate him with a plastic bag, he had been severely beaten, had had wires attached to his genitals and had been electrocuted, and his scrotum had been hung in a draw that was slammed shut.

I asked him why he would now tell me the truth. Xolile said that he knew he did not have long to live and that he was in prison for life. Xolile had another attempted murder charge pending prior to his arrest for the murder of Anni Dewani. He would never be free again.

Zola Tonga called Qwabe while Xolile was with him. Zola said that there was a husband who wanted his wife killed. Zola asked how much this would cost. Qwabe and Xolile conferred and Xolile suggested R15 000.

Xolile said that Qwabe drove Vanda's vehicle, but that Vanda was also in the vehicle. Qwabe and Xolile got out the vehicle and Vanda was told to wait for the husband and drop him off in Khayelitsha at Harare.

Xolile said after he ordered the vehicle to stop at gunpoint, they told Shrien Dewani to get out of the vehicle and directed him to where Vanda was waiting to drop him off in Khayelitsha. Xolile emptied Shrien Dewani's pockets and took R4 000 in cash. Anni Dewani was too terrified to speak or move; Xolile didn't think she was aware that her husband was involved.

They then drove further and dropped off Zola Tonga. Zola told them the money was behind the front passenger seat. Xolile said he was trying to rape Anni when the gun he was holding went off accidentally. It had been his intention to kill her after he had raped her. A witness also stated that she saw Anni's body in the VW Sharran, and that her underwear was below her knees and her dress was pulled up. This was later dismissed in court.

Qwabe and Xolile split the money, but Xolile said he only got R800 for the sale of the jewels; Qwabe kept the rest. Qwabe sold some jewels to a South African actress from a popular local television series who lived nearby where the vehicle was found with Anni Dewani's body inside.

A former employee of the Cape Grace overheard Shrien discussing telephonically with someone that he wanted the jewels back. When I spoke to Paul Hendrikse he told me he had searched Xolile's shack and found only the mobile of Zolo.

The jewels were initially sold to the South African actress, but was returned the next day and hidden in the roof of the shack when it was realised how high profile the case was. I gave the police this information but they could not track her down, but yet a journalist told me that he had interviewed her. Xolile told me they sold the jewels to her, and she lives a few shacks down from where the vehicle with Annie's body inside was discovered.

There is another ring that was sold to a Nigerian shopkeeper in Woodstock, a suburb near Cape Town's city centre.

Shrien Dewani's mobile phone was never found and speaking to my contact in Brandvlei proved unsuccessful.

Xolile showed a thumbs up sign when he got sentenced for life. This is the salute of the 26s gang, which Xolile is known to be a member of. He would have received high ranking for this killing and he would be well looked after by other 26s in prison.

Xolile told me that he wanted to leave the number, but the only way you leave is by dying; there is only one person alive today who miraculously survived the gang's death sentence – he is a former general in the 28s gang.

Xolile is now almost permanently confined to the hospital wing of the prison, where he receives on-going treatment. Some sources claim that he has less than six months to live. Xolile is awaiting trial for attempted murder prior to the killing of Anni Dewani.

I don't think that Xolile regrets his actions, as he talks about it rather nonchalantly. I do not see why Xolile would lie to me now; why admit to attempted rape and murder only now? Is it a death bed confession?

Quotes from Xolile during our interview;

"Zola called Qwabe and I about a man who wanted a woman killed"

"The job was to kill a foreigner's wife and make it look like a hijacking"

"I said we should charge R15 000"

"I was the trigger man"

"Anni was too terrified to speak or move"

"I do not think that she knew her husband was involved"

"The gun went off accidently while I was trying to rape her"

"I was going to kill her after I raped her"

"We arranged transport for the husband after we hijacked the vehicle, there was a car waiting for him"

"We sold some of the jewellery to a South African actress"

"We sold one of her rings to a Nigerian black market dealer"

I met with my lawyer and was referred to Captain Paul Hendrikse of the Hawks organised crime unit and gave him all the new information I received from Xolile.

Shrien Dewani said that Anni Dewani was the love of his life. Yet Anni Dewani was said to want to break off the engagement three times due to Shrien's lack of sexual performance. Shrien said that it was due to hormone treatment he was receiving for infertility.

A senior parliamentary figure claims he had kinky gay sex with Shrien Dewani at a gay fetish club, The Hoist, in London. Another man, a German male prostitute called Leopold Leisser made similar claims and said that Shrien Dewani had paid him for kinky sex on three occasions. Leisser claimed Dewani had told him he needed to 'find a way out of getting married'.

Shrien Dewani had a conversation with Zola Tonga for seventeen minutes outside the Cape Grace Hotel, where he asked Zola if he knew someone who was a hit man; he wanted a woman killed.

Zola contacted Mbolombo, who put Zola in touch with Qwabe and Xolile. The price for the murder was set at R15 000, 00. Shrien wanted to pay in US dollars, but Zola refused and drove Shrien to a Bureau de Change. Zola took Shrien to a black market currency exchange and exchanged $1 500. It was agreed that Zola and the male passenger would be ejected from the vehicle and the female passenger would thereafter be killed. Zola was to receive R5 000 for his part in the plot, but only got paid R1 000 by Shrien.

Shrien suggested that they call their respective families that evening, and, while Anni was speaking with her family in Sweden, Shrien met with Zola to make final arrangements for the murder that night. Zola picked up the Dewanis that evening and drove them in the direction of Strand.

On the way there, Shrien sent Zola a text message to say that the murder had to take place that evening. After the couple had eaten at a restaurant, and on their way driving back to the kidnapping point, Zola sent Shrien a text message asking where the money was. Shrien replied with: 'in an envelope in a pouch behind the passenger seat'.

Shrien said that they were driven around for forty minutes before he got ejected out of the back window of the moving vehicle – why would they do this? This space is small; it would surely draw a lot more attention.

Shrien did not have a scratch on him. He allegedly met with Zola Tonga twice in his taxi in the car park of the Cape Grace Hotel, where he procured a hit man. Dewani apparently had a series of meetings with Zola in the hotel. He was seen handing Zola a package of cash on 16 November 2010, having just moments earlier been sitting next to his grieving father-in-law.

Zola was then recorded entering the toilets and counting the money. Shrien's brother, Preyan Dewani, tried to obtain video footage of Zola and Shrien meeting.

The police have all the phone records and exchange of texting between Zola and Shrien. There is evidence that will be brought to trial that will prove that Dewani orchestrated the murder of his wife.

The murder of Anni Dewani shocked all and created very negative feelings in South Africa, and, shortly thereafter, tourism took a dip.

South Africans are generally in agreement: bring Shrien Dewani to South Africa and let him prove his innocence. If your partner was killed and you were implicated, would it not be your first priority to prove your innocence?

Shrien Dewani's legal team have been fighting his extradition from the word go.

Let him return to South Africa and prove us all wrong. I believe he will get a fair trial.

South Africa is known for its crime, but those who commit crime are always brought to justice no matter how slow the wheels of justice turn.

The following is an impact statement by Anni Dewani's father in court at the trial of Xolile Mngeni.

'Her death, just two weeks after her marriage, has caused me and my family a lot of pain. One day we are happily celebrating her marriage in India and only two weeks later we find out that she has been brutally murdered. Words cannot describe how painfully difficult it has been for us; for myself, my wife, my two other children and the rest of our family.

'Since Anni's death, I have not been able to go back to work. I have not worked for more than two years now. It has been impossible for me to concentrate and, with my profession (electrician); I need full concentration when I work. Thoughts of Anni have always been affecting my concentration and the fact that I am sad and angry. I have been visiting a psychiatrist once every two weeks to help me get my life together and back to normal, but it's a long journey and has been very hard for me.

'The nights have been really hard. My wife and I both struggle to sleep. For one and a half years, we woke up in the middle of the night/early morning at 3 to 4 o' clock and started talking to each other about Anni. We cried and it is just impossible to comfort each other since both of us share the same pain. Also, my son, Anish; I have not seen joy on his face for two years. He has taken this very hard and is full of anger. And my daughter, Ami, she has such sadness in her eyes even though she tries to be really strong. I myself am in an emotional state and have not been able to be there for them.'

I would like to apologise to the Hindocha family if I cause them any further hurt or pain. I believe that any new information should be shared, so that the truth may prevail.

Shrien Dewani is not guilty of any crime until proven so in a court of law.

The General

Death Sentence

I was born on a wine farm in Constantia, Cape Town. My parents both worked in the vineyards and part of their weekly wage was five litres of wine each.

On weekends there were always parties going on in our house, which would always end in violence. I cannot recall a time when my mother did not have a blue eye or split lip. I had three brothers and two sisters and often there was not enough food to feed us. We slept outside in the cold on many occasions, because our parent's friends had priority.

I was ten years old when they separated and because I was the youngest had to go and live with my dad in Ladies Mile. Things weren't much better there and I started stealing the milkman's money tokens from the bottles left in front of homes and exchanged them for half the value in cash.

By the age of twelve I was selling newspapers at the traffic lights with some newfound friends, who were a bit older than me. My dad wasn't aware of this, and one day I did not return home but opted to sleep on the streets with my friends.

Sniffing glue kept us warm at night and through the cold winter days we cuddled up in cardboard boxes in shop entrances. Some of my friends used to go with older white men, who picked them up for sex – upon their return we always had money for glue, cigarettes and food. I never did this and wasn't aware of what they were up to until many years later.

I got caught shoplifting and the police took me home to my father, who told police that he thought I had been with my mother for the past three months. I continued seeing my friends, and was their watch when they did some housebreaking, not long after I used to climb through open windows and unlock doors for them.

I got caught shoplifting wine when I was fifteen and was sentenced to six cuts by the police, for two days after the punishment I still could not walk and it was a month before my wounds healed.

A year later I got caught stealing a hand bag and I sat in Moorland Street jail for four months before my father fetched me and told me in no uncertain terms that this was the last time he would come for me.

When I got out I bought two machetes which I carried under my coat, I took revenge on anyone who had done me wrong in my past. My nick name was 'Wake Up' because when the police saw me, I'd duck and dive and roll on the ground while they were trying to shoot me. They always missed.

I turned eighteen and got arrested for GBH (grievous bodily harm) and housebreaking. The police connected wires to my genitals and shocked me; they beat and jumped on me. I was sentenced to four years at Pollsmoor prison.

I was approached by the numbers and asked which camp I wanted to join or I could become a wyfie. I decided to join the 28s and was their soldier. I was schooled in the number 28.

You are taught that you have no other family in or out of prison, only the 28s. There is only one door in and no door out when you join a number. I always knew this way was wrong but I believed and trusted the number. **John 8:44 You are the children of your father, the Devil, and you want to follow your father's desires. From the very beginning he was a murderer and has never been on the side of truth, because there is no truth in him. When he tells a lie, he is only doing what is natural to him, because he is a liar and the father of all lies.**

I was sent to Allandale prison in Paarl and here I shared a cell with twenty other 28s. Here we got the order from a General to kill another number, but before the hit I was transferred back to Pollsmoor because I was a training carpenter. The hit was executed. At the time the death penalty was still in place in South Africa, nine of the men got hanged and eleven got life sentences.

I escaped with my life for the first time. God had other plans for me. I became a trustee and used to take lunch to the wardens outside the prison gates. On my return I'd pick up a dagga parcel in a prearranged location and carry it back into prison.

I had three months of my sentence left when I walked back into the prison one day and a warden looked inside the pot and found the dagga. The warden asked for leniency and I got five years with a twelve-month suspended sentence, I also had to sign a document for a nine-to-fifteen-year suspended sentence. After twelve months I got a reduced sentence and was released.

When I was released three of us in the number got the order to kill a man. You have to do what you are ordered or there are consequences. We went to a bar in Wynberg and had a drink. A man came up to and said 'Wake Up, I am a detective', and he started searching me. He found two stops of dagga and two knives in my duffel coat. I pulled out a knife I'd hidden in the back of my trousers and fatally stabbed him in the stomach. I left the bar and was a hunted man.

I stabbed many strangers for no reason without feeling any remorse.

I went looking for my mother who was now working on a wine farm in Stellenbosch. She was overjoyed to see me. I said I'd be there for a month, and the following day it was my birthday. My Mom said: 'Son you are thirty years old tomorrow and for the past fifteen years you spent every birthday in jail, so tomorrow I am going to bake you a cake'.

That evening all the workers were having a party, smoking

185

dagga and drinking wine. I pretended to take a puff from the pipe when it was passed to me and when no one was looking I would throw the wine on the floor.

One of the guys asked what I was doing. I had one huge hit of the dagga pipe and remember what a beautiful evening it was, I looked up at the moon and stars and thought how small we were in the universe and these things were bigger than us, God made this. **Genesis 2:1-4 And so the whole universe was completed. By the seventh day God finished what he had been doing and stopped working. He blessed the seventh day and set it apart as a special day, because by that day he completed his creation and stopped working. And that is how the universe was created.**

The next morning was my birthday and I was looking forward to my cake and birthday. I woke up and tried to open my eyes, but they were swollen shut. I was in a police cell in Wynberg, seventy kilometres away. I could not remember anything.

Things started getting clearer later that morning. There was tik in the dagga pipe I'd taken a huge hit from the previous evening. Someone told me about a doctor's house nearby and that he was away on holiday at the time. I broke into the house and found the safe. By now I was an experienced safe cracker. I opened the safe and filled a satchel full of jewels, and as I walked outside I saw blue police lights flashing everywhere. I had triggered a silent alarm.

I ran back into the house and found two samurai swords on a wall. I ran outside like a ninja, screaming, ready to attack. A policeman stood in front of me with his gun aimed at me and said 'Drop your weapons or I will shoot'. I took a swing with one of the swords, aiming at his head. He lifted his arm while stepping back and I sliced off the buttons on his sleeve. He jumped forward and slammed the metal butt of the gun in my face.

I remember being hit with batons and kicked until I lost consciousness. I was charged with housebreaking and attempted murder. I was in my cell in pain and when the policemen checked on me, I asked for pain killers. They asked how many I wanted, I said 'five' and they punched me in the face five times.

I had a suspended sentence of nine to fifteen years including the two charges as I now stood in court. But God intervened again. During the identity parade the policeman I'd attacked stopped and looked directly at me but did not identify me. Also I was born Matthews but when I left prison on the previous occasion they gave me an ID book (South African Identity document) that said Koopman, so all my previous sentences were under the surname of Matthews.

The magistrate asked if this was my first offence and I said yes. I was sent to Pollsmoor while awaiting sentence, and as I walked out of court I saw the scale of justice and a realisation and a feeling of peace overcame me. I was no longer afraid. I did not want to be a number anymore. This was the beginning of the hell I was about to endure.

I had worked my way up to a General in the 28s and prison time for me would be easy, but on our arrival in the holding cell you are asked which camp you belong to. There were four new arrivals and I told the numbers that I was a Frans and they told me to stand one side.

There were eleven 26s in the cell and they came over to me again and asked if I was a number and I said no, I'm a Frans. The following evening there was a numbers court case in the cell and the 26s gave me the death penalty, handed down by the 28s through prison negotiation.

The death penalty would entail me getting killed first in any manner possible, then my head would be severed and forced into the bars of the cell door, the rest of my body would be cut up into flushable pieces, then my bones would be broken and smashed and flushed down the toilet, even the femur and bigger bones are put against a wall and broken and then smashed into finer pieces.

In the morning when the officers arrive all they find is your head.

One of the 26s came over to me and told me to get out of the cell, any which way I could. I was isolated and had to sit alone because nobody wanted to be associated with me. I started praying for the first time in my life, the only prayer I knew was 'The Lord's Prayer'

Matthew 6:9-13
Our Father, who art in heaven,
Hallowed be thy name;
Thy kingdom come;
Thy will be done on earth as it is in heaven.
Give us this day our daily bread;
And forgive us our trespasses
As we forgive those who trespass against us;
And lead us not into temptation,
But deliver us from evil.
For the kingdom, the power, and the glory are yours
Forever and forever. Amen.

This for me is the most powerful prayer, because Jesus told us this is how we should pray. One of the Franse gave me twenty pages of a bible to use as cigarette paper. I was too afraid to go to the toilet and for the first three days I pissed my pants. I stopped eating and drinking. I just smoked the bible. I lost so much weight that I could put my hands around my waist.

After two and a half weeks, the one 26 came up to me again and said 'Please get yourself out of this cell'. The prison officers came in for inspection and I knew I had to do something now because my death was imminent. We had to stand in a line in the cell while we were inspected. One of the wardens stopped in front of me and I tried to speak but I could not, it felt like my lips were glued shut. When they left the cell I tried to move in their direction but my feet would not move, then they were gone and a feeling of dread overcame me. I knew that this was the night I was going to die, it was the 26 of the month.

Jeremiah 29:11-12 "I alone know the plans I have for you, plans to bring you prosperity and not disaster, plans to bring about the future you hope for, then you will call me. You will come and pray to me, and I will answer you".

The 26s sat in a circle that evening, then three stood up and the man who had pleaded with me was in front. They were all carrying knives. They had to execute the sentence or get killed themselves. The 26 that had pleaded with me only had a nine-month sentence, the other two men had one hundred and fifty and two hundred years in prison , the latter two had nothing to lose.

This night I was going to die. I was sitting with my hands on my head praying, I saw the knives raised, I shut my eyes for an instant and when I opened them the three men were laying on the floor. They went back to the circle and a fourth man, the Captain, jumped up and said 'wit bene (death) vanaand moet hy dood wees' (tonight he must be dead).

The fourth man approached me, I was still sitting with my hands on my head saying the lord's prayer. He approached me and tried to stab me but the knife could not penetrate me and he too fell on the ground in a daze. I closed my eyes and then they were all back in the circle. In the morning I pinched myself, I was confused, was I dead was I mad? **John 3:16 "Then, this, is how we will know that we belong to the truth; this is how we will be confident in God's presence"**.

I felt the tears run down my cheeks and a warm feeling spreading from my feet to my sides up to my head and back again, a feeling of comfort that is hard to describe. I said 'God I open my heart to you'. I cried and could not stop, it was tears of joy. The 26 shouted from the corner 'Dit help nie jy huil nie want vanaand kry jy wit bene' (It does not help crying because tonight you die). I wasn't afraid, it felt like I had been in a deep sleep and just woken up. It felt like the scales had fallen from my eyes and now I could see the truth.

That evening the 26s were sitting in their circle again, I walked up to them and asked if I could pray, they laughed at me. I said to them I was like Daniel in the lion's den and that they could not kill me, if God was for me, who could be against me.

Some of the Franse started singing hymns out of the bible, one of the 26s had tears in his eyes and I saw a message in his eyes. I'd never been to church before but started quoting from the bible. The men in the cell asked why I hadn't told them I was a pastor. I said I wasn't, but God had plans for me. I had the best sleep that night for the first time in three weeks.

The following morning when I awoke, some of the men came up to me and jumped back and called everyone in the cell to come over to see what had happened to me. My eyes, including my pupils, had turned bright yellow. The men walking past the cell on their way to court asked for me to touch them and pray for them. Everyone I touched that day went home.

Many years later I am still in touch with the 26 that tried to kill me. Some of the other 26s in that cell were all killed by their own number or hanged. I am the only known number to survive a death sentence since the number began in 1812.

I was transferred to a single cell with two other men. A prison officer handed me a small pocket bible which I started reading. I could recite many verses out the bible without ever having read the bible before. I joke and tell people it is perhaps that I smoked so many pages from the bible that it must be ingrained in me.

Then a young 26 called James was placed in my cell, he wanted to change his life and turn to God.

I was introduced to James recently and he told me this story, I knew everything he told me was the truth, because the General confirmed it.

I grew up in Piketberg on the West Coast. I had a privileged upbringing and got everything I wanted. My father went to prison when my mother was still pregnant, she remarried a few years later.

190

I was of small stature and got bullied at school constantly. It made me very unhappy and my parents could not understand the reasons for my mood swings. I never had any friends in school and hardly spoke to anyone.

When I was ten years old I started looking up to gangsters, they took me under their wing and they sorted out all the boys bullying me. They gave me their guns to look after and I kept it in my school bag, and gave it to them when they needed it. I started smoking dagga and then mandrax.

The people in my school started looking up to me because I was always hanging out with the gangsters who were much older than me. My mannerisms changed and I started feeling invincible.

I asked the gangsters what I had to do to join them because I saw their nice cars, cash and the pretty girls always hanging around them. They told me to wait until the time was right then I had to offer something closest to me. I continued running with them, using and selling drugs for the Americans.

I had just turned seventeen when one Saturday afternoon I was in the kitchen and I started arguing with my mother. My stepfather walked into the kitchen and said: 'Peter do not speak to your mother like that'. I walked into the backyard and he followed. I threw an orange at him and he ducked and said 'Missed'. I said to him: 'Maak van my n poes dan maak ek van jou a poes' (Make a fool out of me and I will make a fool out of you).

I pulled out a knife and stabbed him repeatedly, until he collapsed to the ground and stopped breathing. I went to the gangsters and showed them the blood stained knife and said 'This I offer to join you'. They gave me a change of clothes and hid me in a house.

The police caught up with me a few weeks later and I was sent to young offenders awaiting trial. I was here a week when I stabbed one of the other inmates in the neck and almost killed him.

I now faced a murder charge and one of attempted murder. I was sent to medium B at Piketberg prison and spent two years there for the murder of my stepfather and was released.

I went to court for the attempted murder charge and got fined R30 000 or two years' incarceration. I had no money and was preparing to go to prison when my gangster brothers bailed me out. I was told that I had to pay for this debt by killing one of the members of the Fancy Boys Gang. I found Romeo walking down the street and shot him point blank in the chest he died instantly. The guys bought me new clothes and took me to a Spur Steakhouse for a meal as a reward.

I shot and killed another man whose drug turf I wanted to take over, he was a 28. I started dealing from two houses and bought my tik directly from the drug factories, which was in the centre of Langebaan and Vredenberg. I used to watch them make the tik and sometimes rat poison and battery acid was part of the ingredients.

I had many police friends whom I used to supply with drugs and women. I could get any file or docket and I even had magistrates I could bribe, but depending on the policeman or court, sometimes things did not quite work that way. I defrauded a bank of R50 000 and got sentenced to eighteen months in Pollsmoor prison.

When I got to Pollsmoor the numbers had already heard about me, I was a 26 Frans and indicated that I wanted to join their number. The Glass of the number 26s was watching me, he had to see how I interacted with other people. Then The Njangi (numbers Doctor) told me to strip, he looked for any other number tattoos and had to see if I had any afflictions, if you have a lost eye or crippled hand or any disability then you cannot join the 26s. I passed this test.

Then six numbers asked me if I was ready for the rules, I saluted and said yes. The schooled me in the way of the 26 from my boots to my helmet. I had just turned eighteen. After six days I was ready and got the command to stab a prison officer.

There were two of us new recruits and we had to work together. I stabbed a prison officer in the neck. The man with me took the knife and handed it to some prison officers. They sent him to some single cells.

The prison officers then set the dogs on me and beat me nearly to death, even when I was lying in my hospital bed, they would come and hit me and spit in my face. The doctors were no better, they would not give me pain killers, I would cry for days in pain. When I came out of the prison hospital I was respected in my cell and was made Inspector one.

I could not walk properly for two months. I spent a few years in prison and then was released on parole.

On my release I opened another two drug houses where I also had women who worked for me as prostitutes.

I would meet a girl in a pub or club. I had lots of money, a nice car and this always impressed the girls. I would take them to the finest restaurants and buy them gifts for the first month. Then I'd smoke tik in front of them and tell them to try it just once.

Tik is highly addictive and if not after the first hit then the second try, you are hooked. Now the girls would not have much money and when they had nothing left to give, I'd tell them they have to start working for me. Many of the girls came from good families and lived locally. I would take them to work in other areas or in a brothel somewhere.

I would use these girls to befriend rich girls in clubs and pubs all over Cape Town, spoil them with drinks and meals out and introduce them to me and then it was the same routine again. I had thirty girls of all races working for me.

There was this white girl who was twenty and came from a good family background. I got her hooked on tik and she worked for me for about three months all over Cape Town. One evening she was sitting with me at one of the houses and we smoked some tik. I'd noticed whenever she was around me, she used to send text messages. I had linked her phone without her knowledge to mine to see who she was texting.

She was working as an informant for the police. I gave the order and some of my men stabbed her to death with a broken beer bottle and dumped the body into a rubbish bin naked, left with only a tik lolly on her.

I had many policemen working with me and often we'd smoke tik together. I bought guns and bullets from them and they would inform me of any drug bust. I'd called them from my mobile and organise firearm licences and get dockets to disappear.

I went to Cape Town one weekend and got into an argument in a bar and I stabbed a guy in his anus three times. I got arrested and was sentenced to Drakenstein prison for two years. I was an Inspector in the number and just integrated back into prison life. I got the order to kill a 26 who betrayed our number. We get locked down from three in the afternoon until six the following morning, so there is lots of time to do what we wanted. There were six of us in the cell with the condemned man – he was twenty-two years old.

I cut his throat, then we cut off his head and placed it in the bars of the cell door, there is another solid steel door beyond that. We cut his body into flushable pieces and then broke all his bones into small pieces until that could be flushed as well, the femurs and bigger bones were placed against the wall and jumped on until this was also flushable, when this was all done and cleaned up there was only one thing left to do. We kept his heart and cut it into six pieces and ate it, he was our blood but now his blood and memory would walk with us. I felt no remorse.

I did not get prosecuted for this crime but some of the other men did, I was released after a year and went back to my old ways.

I used to walk past a particular house in my neighbourhood where a woman in her fifties lived. Her name was Aunt Sophie. We always greeted each other and soon we were talking and became friends. She became my confidante and I felt I could tell her anything and I did. She had a daughter who was the same age as me, Melanie, and soon the two of us were dating. I asked Aunt

Sophie if it was okay if I could date her daughter and she gave me her blessing even though she knew my history.

I loved Melanie but would spend weeks away at a time in my drug dens and often with other women. I felt really bad, bought an expensive ring and proposed to Melanie, she agreed and I was the happiest man in the world.

Melanie had a daughter from a previous relationship, Becky, who was five years old. When Melanie heard that I was a gangster and drug dealer, she broke off our engagement, saying that she had to look out for her daughter. I was living in the house at this point and now had to move.

I was sitting in the back yard contemplating what to do next and then I pulled out my gun and placed it in my mouth. But I could not pull the trigger, I repeated this for three hours but could not do it. I was not afraid but an inner voice said to me that it would be wrong. I went out that evening and robbed and shot a stranger.

When I got home I asked Aunt Sophie to look after the gun for me like she had done on many occasions. I had a court appearance the following day for an assault charge and was sentenced to Pollsmoor for twelve months.

I was put in a cell with fellow 26s and an order came from the Generals that they wanted a prison officer killed and if I did this then I would become a General.

I had had enough of crime and wanted to get out of this hell that I'd been living in but knew there was no way out. I heard about the General they call the Pastor, who survived the death sentence and I wanted to know more about this man.

I found out that he was in another section, I had some prison officers on my payroll and arranged to get transferred to his cell. I spoke to him at length about my life and he told me that he was indeed a General that used to hand down death sentences but now he worked for God and would hand down eternal life sentences in the name of Jesus Christ. I gave my life to God in a prison cell in

Pollsmoor. **John: 31-32 "If you continue in my word, then are you my disciples indeed; and you shall know the truth, and the truth shall make you free"**

The General: I guided one person back to Christ and now many prisoners were calling me Pastor. I wanted to learn the bible more and teach the word of God but didn't know where to start, I opened the bible and stopped at **Revelation 1:12-20"I turned around to see who was talking to me and I saw seven gold lamp stands, and among them there was what looked like a human being, wearing a robe that reached to his feet, and a gold belt around his chest.**

His hair was white as wool, or as snow, and his eyes blazed like fire; his feet shone like brass that had been refined and polished, and his voice sounded like a roaring waterfall. He held seven stars in his right hand, and a sharp two-edged sword came from his mouth. His face was bright as the midday sun.

When I saw him, I fell down at his feet like a dead man. He placed his right hand on me and said, Don't be afraid! I am the first and the last. I am the living one! I was dead, but now I am alive for ever and ever. I have authority over death and the world of the dead. Write, then, the things you see, both the things that are now and the things that will happen afterwards.

This is the secret meaning of the seven stars that you see in my right hand, and the seven gold lamp-stands; the seven stars are the angels of the seven churches, and the seven lamp-stands are the seven churches. I'd dreamt about this before.

One evening as I lay in my bed, suddenly in a vision I saw a white and brown cat, and it walked over my chest and its tail wrapped around my neck, then it disappeared.

My feet started getting freezing cold and then it went up my legs all the way up to my chest, I was afraid and said: 'God please forgive me for all my sins'. The cold had reached my neck and then moved down my body, out at my feet and my whole body was bathed in a warm golden glow. I realised that this was my spiritual death and resurrection in the flesh.

Prison is very noisy and I could not concentrate when reading the bible. I prayed and all sound around me seemed to disappear, I was so deep in thought that the food trolley had passed my cell. I prayed and said 'God I need food' and a few minutes later the man with the food trolley came back to my cell, which they never do, and gave me food. There were lots of miracles that happened to me and every time I asked God for anything spiritual or physical I received it.

I was transferred to Robben Island in 1978. I was in the van from Pollsmoor to the harbour when a young 26 told me to give him my shoes. I took them off and he threw me his old shoes, and asked if I was going to tell on him. I said: 'If you really want and need my shoes you can have them'. I had learned to turn the other cheek. The man gave me my shoes back.

We boarded a ship called the Dias, where we were taken to the hull at the bottom of the ship and chained down. One of the men pointed to me and said: 'You are going to get killed'. I said 'No they will not kill me, I walk with God'.

We were strip-searched when we arrived on Robben Island and the prison officers saw my tattoos. They saw that I was a 28 and said to me, here your number doesn't work, we will put the dogs on you and feed you to the sharks.

I told them I was a man of God. They put me in a cell and the numbers searched us. They asked who I was and I told them I was a man of God. They said they'd heard about me and that I would die the next day.

The next day we were put to work in the prison yard picking up rubbish. One of the prison officers said: 'You come with me to clean the dog cages, all the dogs are out'. All the cages were empty and I had to remove all the dog faeces and wash the cages out.

The last cage had a lock on but it was unlocked. I removed the lock and started cleaning the cage. As I moved to the back of the cage, in front of me was a huge Alsatian and it was growling at me. I froze for an instant in terror and then slowly started backing out the cage. The dog followed me step for step, until I got out the cage and shut the gate. I could not believe that I got out the cage.

When the prison officer returned I asked him why they hadn't told me that there was a dog in the cage. The warden took me with his vehicle to where the other officers were gathering. They asked me where was I born and if I was real, because I should be dead. I replied: 'I am a child of God and he protects me'. The next day I was made a trustee and sent to work at the prison officers houses.

I arrived the next morning at one of the houses and knocked on the door. A woman opened, invited me in and told me to sit down. She left the house and returned with six other women, she brought me tea and biscuits and asked me to tell them about God.

I gave them my testimony and started quoting from the bible, after a few hours I told them I'd better start cleaning or I would be in trouble, they told me to stay where I was and gave me more tea and sandwiches and started cleaning the house. One woman asked me whether it was a sin to lie in bed and pray, instead of kneeling next to the bed. I said that although it was better to kneel, you can pray to God where ever and whenever you wanted, God would bless you regardless.

This continued for a month, drinking tea and talking about God while the woman cleaned, I felt truly blessed. I was moved to another work party and it was another trustee time to work the houses. The prison officers heard I was spreading the word of God and moved me to a new cell every two weeks.

One night an aggressive youngster approached me in the cell and told me to give him my sugar, because the bible says you should give. I only had one small bag but gave it to him, the next day I found three bags of sugar on my bed. I was truly blessed.

I was walking with my hands behind my back one day when

a prison officer came up to me and said: 'Do you think you are walking on your father's farm'. I said 'Yes this is all God's farm'. He ripped my trustee badge off my uniform and threw it on the ground. I told him it was ok, and that I had another one. He asked me very threateningly where it was. I replied it was in my heart.

Another time there was a dying man in a cell. I went and prayed for him, he was unconscious and had the death rattle, suddenly he grabbed my hand and placed it on his head and I continued praying. He jumped up and was healed through the grace of God.

There was a man who came from Port Elizabeth who was the leader of the Mafia's gang. He was in for murder and got the death sentence. He came to me and asked me to pray with him because he wanted to be like me, he accepted God but did nothing as in works or proclaiming the word of God, we started spending a lot of time together worshipping together, and he became a disciple for God.

I saw Nelson Mandela from a distance on a few occasions but never met him, because political prisoners were segregated from normal prisoners. I was walking near the kitchen one day when I passed a group of 26s. They said to me: 'Wit bene' (death). I walked up to them and said 'I am not your brother'. **Jeremiah 15: 19-21 To this the lord replied "If you return, I will take you back, and you will be my servant again. If instead of talking nonsense you proclaim a worthwhile message, you will be my prophet again. The people will come back to you, and you will not need to go to them. I will make you like a solid bronze wall as far as they are concerned. They will fight against you, but they will not defeat you. I will be with you to protect you and keep you safe. I will rescue you from the power of the wicked and violent people. I the Lord have spoken.**

There were some Franse there peeling potatoes. I took six knives from them and handed it to the 26s and said 'You can kill me, but wait until I pray and when I say amen then you can kill me, and remember God loves you and if it his will then so be it and I still love you'.

I started praying and when I said amen they all had their hands on their sides. I took the knives from them and handed it back to the Franse. I told them: 'You must give your heart to God or go to hell, that is your free will'.

The men all came to me over time and asked me to pray for them, the ones that didn't do it in prison, did it on the outside and wrote and told the men still inside.

On another occasion some 26s and 28s were stabbing each other, I jumped on the table and said 'In the name of Jesus Christ I command you to stop' – they all did and were taken away by prison officers.

I spent most of my youth in prison and it got me nothing for all the crimes I committed. Prison in South Africa is harsh and unfortunately once you have been in once, your chances of rehabilitation are very slim.

I found God and was saved. I have spent the last ten years at various prisons in the Western Cape telling people about the glory of God, I have with the grace of God saved many men, you have to replace your evil for good, you have to choose.

I have become good friends with Pastor Koopman and see him on a regular basis. He has done a lot of good work in South Africa but now he has a vision to spread his story worldwide, and save more lives. I believe his dream will come true very soon. His repeats the same words every time I see him: God saved my life, now I will help others to save theirs.

Is it you God?

I listen to people every day, and wonder if the truth may come my way
   The gangsters, addicts and lost searching for God or so they say
   I look at their hearts and wonder if it is the truth they search for today
   I know sometimes it is hard because once in a while we all question God
   I ask God if they can be saved, they say they are sorry
   He says not to worry; today they will only take the first step
   Then after a while I will put their souls to rest
   The Devil is angry he has lost too many, he will win them back because God is his enemy
   Satan will remind them of the pleasures of tik and the lines of coke that they sniffed
   Maybe I will be saved today, what do you think? Or maybe I should just have another drink
   Working for God is so hard, but anything is better than a prison yard
   We will change our lives they say, but just not today
   Because God is forgiving, and made me this way
   When I pray he will listen and bless me when I say I am a Christian
   God says that is not good enough and soon I will call your bluff
   But I know it is up to me who I choose and if it is Satan I loose
   There is a little more time to do one more crime
   There is no more time I tell you on the final chime!
   Who do you pray to? Is it to God or Satan?
   Dennis Heyns

Conclusion

South Africa is one of the most violent countries in the world, but every big city in the world has crime and violence. According to crime statistics for the 2012/13 financial year released by the South African Police Service, the Western Cape recorded a 10 percent increase in violent crimes, as murder, robberies and assaults rose to new highs.

A total of 2 580 people were murdered in the province over the past year, amounting to just more than seven murders a day. And while the Western Cape recorded dramatic spikes in its crime levels, it still trails behind Gauteng, the Eastern Cape and KwaZulu-Natal when it comes to murders.

KwaZulu-Natal is still the most violent province, with over 3 600 murders committed there. The Eastern Cape recorded 3 344 murders, and Gauteng came in at 2 997.

South Africa's murder rate is therefore about four and a half times higher than the global average of 6.9 murders per 100 000.

Rape statistics in the country were flawed because, under the category of sexual crimes, rape was lumped together with non-violent crimes such as prostitution. A woman is raped in South Africa every twenty-six seconds, only one in twenty-five women report being raped.

I believe that the majority of the South African Police Service (SAPS) is not corrupt and provides great service. But a two-year audit of the South African Police Service's 157 500 members show 1 448 of them had been convicted of crimes.

The SAPS revealed recently that 1 448 serving police officers were convicted criminals, among them a major-general, ten brigadiers, 21 colonels, ten majors, 43 lieutenant-colonels, 163 captains, 84 lieutenants and 716 warrant officers.

And it has hesitantly promised to rid the police of these 'unwanted elements' by June 2014.

Among them, a police chief was found to be taking bribes from a drug dealer and in another incident a policeman was caught on tape pimping a policewoman to a man in a mall parking lot, 768 criminal cases had been filed against police officers. Among these were 516 charges of assault, 50 of murder, 94 of rape, seven of attempted rape and 71 of sexual assault.

I asked a senior police officer who had been in the service for twenty-six years what the problem could be within in the service, why the bad policing, corruption and brutality.

He told me that being a policeman was a calling, you will be overworked and not become rich, and some detectives work on as many as two hundred cases at a time.

Then there was the integration of former Umkhonto we Sizwe (MK, translated as "Spear of the Nation", the former military wing of the ANC) soldiers who fought against the apartheid regime into the police service, who have no policing background and who'd been given high police officer rankings.

So why do so many policemen take bribes, let us also look at their monthly income and remember that every day they put their lives at risk, but some would gladly turn a blind eye for as little as R20.00

Constable	R 6 200
Sergeant	R9 960
Warrant Officer	R12 490
Captain	R15 800
Lieutenant Colonel	R19 900
Colonel	R36 000

Then you have your higher ranking officers and the income increases accordingly.

The SAPS kill rate is 317 per 100 000 officers. Five times more SA police officers are killed here than in the United States.

The solution may be to fire all SAPS officers police with criminal records and immediately suspend those under investigation.

Testing and the ability of all policemen are vital, race or background should not be a factor. Retraining must be implemented where necessary. The Hawks organised crime unit has its hands full and corruption has also been uncovered in their ranks. A new special task force should be implemented solely to investigate any criminal activities within police ranks.

Income packages have to be restructured, giving policemen a reasonable living wage. Policemen that go beyond the call of duty should be compensated financially and otherwise. The killing of any policeman must be dealt with severely by our courts; they are after all our protectors.

The same applies within correctional services. Prison officers with criminal records and those accepting bribes, an everyday occurrence in South Africa, must be dealt with in the same way as the police. The same benefits should also apply.

The other problem that the prison service has to deal with is a lack of prison officers, it is a known fact that gangsters keep the peace and maintain order in South African prisons and in turn often a blind eye will be turned to their illegal activities.

The South African Correctional Service should also offer attractive packages as to attract more officers. There are prisoners who currently have 200/300/500 years in prison and continue to commit crime including murder in prison.

These prisoners should be isolated and put into solitary confinement twenty-three hours a day. Any person arrested with no criminal record should be segregated from previous offenders, until sentenced; this will prevent rape, intimidation and violence.

In South Africa the only way that serious crime will decrease will be with the death penalty, I know some think this is morally wrong but the majority of South Africans will agree, lets vote on this?

Paedophiles who have repeatedly offended should be chemically castrated. Model prisoners should be rewarded and more work programmes must be put in place. Prisoners are locked up for eighteen hours a day, let prisoners work for their keep. Farming on a large scale is a good start. Educate and train prisoners in some skill. The government must put half way houses in place so that prisoners can be integrated back into society; prisoners often reoffend shortly after release because they have nowhere to go.

Then we have Pagad (People against Gangsterism and Drugs) I interviewed them and this is what I learnt.

Pagad was formed initially by local neighbourhood watches in Cape Town townships with most members being Muslim. People were not happy with what police and government were achieving and Pagad started to expose gangsters and drug dealers, putting pressure on them to stop their activities. Initially Pagad held peaceful demonstrations but increasingly took matters into their own hands.

Pagad supporters gathered at the Gatesville mosque on the evening of 4 August 1996. There were approximately 2 000 members, many armed with firearms, who went to 20 London Road, Salt River, Cape Town. A house known for drug dealing, linked to twins Rashied and Rashaad Staggie, leaders of The Hard Livings gang.

The group asked the brothers to come outside to receive a message, however they were told that they were not at home – the occupants of the house were to afraid to come out. Pagad supporters opened fire on the house. In the chaos that ensued, eighteen Pagad supporters were wounded after being caught in the crossfire of members in their own group.

Rashaad Staggie arrived on the scene while ambulance personal were attending to the wounded. He was pulled out of his vehicle and shots were fired at him. While medical personnel were attending to Rashaad a petrol bomb was thrown at him setting him alight.

He managed to get up and ran towards the house but supporters attacked him with batons, kicked and fired several shots at him. Rashaad Staggie died in the gutter in front of the house.

Rashied Staggie has been in custody in Brandvlei prison since 2003 and was found guilty of giving orders to have a teenage girl kidnapped and gang-raped. He got fifteen years. He ordered the hit on the girl for allegedly having ties with rival gang, the Americans.

While in prison in 2004 he was convicted of stealing weapons from the Faure police armoury and sentenced to a further thirteen years to run concurrently with the rape sentence.

The Western Cape department of correctional services announced that Staggie was to be released on day parole on 23 September 2013.However on the 4 December 2013, he was ordered back to Pollsmoor for breaking his bail conditions.

During his parole release he made headlines when he signed with newly launched political party the Patriotic Alliance, headed by former prisoners Gayton Mackenzie and Kenny Kunene. Staggie was electronically tagged and was believed to have visited several addresses in Mitchell's Plain where police arrested five residents for gun and drug dealing.

Pagad was believed to be not only responsible for the killing of a large number of gang leaders, but also the bombings of synagogues, gay nightclubs – the most prominent being the bombing of the

Planet Hollywood restaurant in Cape Town on 25th August 1998.

Magistrate Pieter Theron, who was presiding in a case involving Pagad members, was murdered in a drive-by shooting in September 2000. It had become clear that Pagad had not become a part of the solution, but part of the problem.

I had a meeting with the spokesperson for Pagad, Cassiem Parker. Cassiem works as a mechanical engineer but spends most of his spare time working with Pagad. Cassiem said he learnt a lot from Pagad. 'I had a limited vision and just stuck to the normal parameters but Pagad taught me to look further than the tip of my nose,' he said. 'Pagad does a lot more than just organising marches, we interact with communities, we ask the individual how they feel, we teach them how to raise children and how to interact with neighbours. We show them that there is more than one way to live your life.

'Pagad was formed in 1995 after many meetings and complaints at the mosque regarding gangsters and drug dealers in the communities. The people had had enough and organised the first march to a drug dealer's house with many more marches to other dealer's houses to follow and demanded that they immediately stop their drug dealing or more serious steps would be taken against him.

'Targeting firstly the smaller dealers and then the bigger fish like Staggie, and to the murderers of Staggie, Pagad says we salute you. Pagad was now working against the paper trail of democracy, organising marches objecting to gangsterism and drugs.

'The ANC (African National Congress) government did not know what to do with Pagad, politicians wanted to give us a platform, but we wanted to work with the government.

'We protested at Cape Town International airport and knew that this was an entry point for drugs. The police arrested 26 Pagad supporters and all got six months house arrest. Spokesperson for the President's office made a statement after this peaceful demonstration, stating that Pagad was no better than any other gang. This is what the government wanted, we knew our time was done and we could no longer depend on the support of the government.

'After this it was extremely difficult to hold demonstrations and even if you were identified as a supporter you were banned from future meetings or risk arrest.

'Police contacted supporters work places and many got fired as employers now did not want to be associated with Pagad. I was called in by two directors of the company I worked for and told that I had to leave Pagad or leave the company, I told them to make the decision.

'A few weeks later the managing director called me in and asked why I was still a member of Pagad, because all others that worked there were no longer members. Most decided to keep a low profile. Then a few months later I was asked to speak with the board and to my surprise they asked me if I could do anything about drug taking by employees within the company. I was not bitter and arranged a counsellor through Pagad.

'We had a meeting in Bloemfontein with some supporters and we were in talks to open a branch. One week later we got a call from the National Intelligence agency and were told to stop any plans to open a branch here or spend the rest of my life in jail.

'The organs of state create the barriers between drug dealers or gangsters; otherwise this problem would have been solved long ago. When a gangster or drug dealer gets killed and they suspect Pagad, it is labelled as crimes against the state. Local police do not get involved – special police and special prosecutors deal with Pagad.

'We approached the police trying to reach a common agenda; we had a few meetings and told them where to find drug dealers and gangsters committing crime. The police said that they had to monitor us when we marched twice a week and therefore did not have the manpower to raid.

'They told us to stop night marches so that they could go and raid. We stopped but the police had during this time got a law passed whereby we had to get their approval of where we could march, and there were no raids.

'This broke the trust and momentum of talks with the police, now the police were not talking to us directly but instead sent their legal service department to continue talks with us. Most members had been previously arrested during marches and South African Police Legal Services said that they did not sit around a table with criminals.

'So once again we were on our own, we would get approached by communities who asked us to come and march in their area. We then would approach the police and ask for permission to march on a particular route, we were refused mostly on the grounds that it passed a gangster or drug dealer's house and this was an invasion of their civil liberty.

'We now had to find a different approach; I have a background to document things meticulously. We had sufficient evidence who and where drug dealers were. Firstly we approach the users, then the small dealers. We go to different ones until we find the importers and big players.

'Pagad has no regrets closing smaller businesses that were connected to dealing drugs, but we rattled their cages and now big businesses turned against us. Many members were imprisoned, just because they would consistently be seen at our meetings. Police pursue members more passionately than any other.

'I can say this because I was involved on the legal side. Even prosecutors said that they had never seen such legal action against individuals. We got big lawyers like the drug dealers, but then the state got special prosecutors.

'Sometimes the interests of justice do not permit release on bail, whether the interests of justice favour release or otherwise. If a drug dealer or gangster is charged with a crime, the court is asked in the interests of justice to grant bail and it is usually granted. If a Pagad member asks to be granted bail in the interests of justice, it is refused.

'There are currently eleven Pagad members in prison. There seems be the same treatment here. When a member applies for parole, documents cannot be found. One member asked his counsellor in prison to help him with his presentation, his documents could not be found and this was postponed for many more months.

'Many Pagad members teach in prison and even have former numbers now working with them. The prison authorities do not approve and in one instance a senior member had seventeen men converted to the Pagad camp, they were all separated and sent to different prisons.

'Pagad have different sponsors and do not want a receipt, most sponsors in any other business will ask for a receipt. This is because once the police had followed some members in a car and pulled them over in Worcester, police confiscated a receipt book and contacted everyone in the book, telling them that they were being watched because they were suspected members.

'Pagad has one paid employee. On Fridays we would sell fruit, veg and other goods outside their centre in Athlone and have a braai (BBQ). We also do other fundraising drives.

'When a tap is running it is pointless to continuously mopping up (Counselling of addicts). Remove the tap all together and the problem is solved (drugs),' said Cassiem.

Cassiem might be right. When the community gets fed up with the SAPS and does not get results, their hand is forced, not that it is necessarily right.

We also have 'Kangaroo' courts in the townships where criminals get punished by the local community. Sometimes with a severe beating or even death. I asked one of the locals why this was done and his reply did not shock or surprise me.

He said rapists and violent criminals can get bail of R500 or less and because the wheels of justice turn so slowly, dockets go missing or a policeman gets paid for a file to disappear. On other occasions victims or witnesses are intimidated. He added that communities did not trust the police, who mix with local gangsters and accept bribes.

Then there's affirmative action and this has proved to be ineffective. People are put in positions which they are not qualified for. We know that radicalized identities, from situations such as Rwanda, Nazi Germany and many others, have genocidal potential.

During the apartheid years there was an over-correction in the direction of the whites, now there is an overcorrection for all non-whites. It will take many years for this to equalise. The new generations of youth were born after the disbandment of apartheid and should be given equal opportunities.

"I have fought against white domination, and I have fought against black domination, I have cherished the ideal of a democratic and free society in which all persons live together in harmony and with equal opportunities. It is an ideal which I hope to live for and to achieve. But if needs be, it is an ideal for which I am prepared to die." **Nelson Mandela**, said at the Rivonia trial before he was sent to prison for twenty-seven years.

I know many men and women who had terrible childhoods, some living from one home to the next; others have had to endure physical and sexual abuse and some were denied the opportunity to get a proper education.

Yet many of these people turn out to be the best success stories. We all have choices, no matter what our circumstances are. Often people do not take responsibility for their actions, but rather blame it on secondary things. It was a violent movie ... I was abused as a child, I was poor and so on.

When a family member or close friend has an alcohol or drug addiction, it is very traumatic for the family to deal with the situation. One thing one has to remember, is addicts and especially drug addicts will lie and steal from anyone that is around them at the time.

Addicts are brilliant manipulators and will convince you that they are clean and need money for a drug debt or anything else barr drugs. To threaten an addict does not work but tough love is definitely the answer. You have to set conditions and boundaries after them completing a stint in rehab. Certain people and places are also to be avoided, one drink, one puff, one pill will not harm you they will be told by 'friends'.

This is a long process and sometimes it takes many years for an addict to rehabilitate. Do not give up on them and be ready for a long battle. You cannot force any addict to rehabilitate, it has to be their decision. You can help, but ultimately they also need to contribute.

Do not give in when they are on the streets and on drugs and tell you that they are hungry and have nowhere to go. They can always find drugs and therefore should always be able to find food. There are many places in all cities and towns where you can get a plate of food. This is war. Do not surrender until you are sure that rehabilitation is what they really want.

Most people have internet access, Google rehabs on how to deal with addicts and even better, join a support group with similar people going through the same thing as you.

Some people do not have the same opportunities and start in life, but this does not stop them becoming the greatest humans to walk on this planet. Helen Keller became deaf, dumb and blind shortly after birth. Despite her great misfortune, she has written her name into the pages of history.

She has proved throughout her life that no one is defeated, until defeat has been accepted as a reality.

Charles Dickens began by pasting labels on blackening pots. Maria Beadnell was the first love of Charles Dickens. Her father Mr Beadnell was a banker. He felt that Charles was too young and lacking in prospects to be considered a serious suitor. This gave Charles Dickens the encouragement and willpower to prove those who doubled him wrong. He became one of the greatest authors of all time. He never did get to married to Maria Beadnell, but he made the world richer and a better place for all who read his books. Disappointments over love affairs generally has the effect of turning men to drink and women to nervous breakdowns, and this is because most people never learn the art of transmuting their strongest emotions into dreams of a constructive nature.

Humans have become lazy; children no longer play outside but rather sit on their computers. Take any train or bus journey and observe your fellow passengers, I guarantee you that more than 50% will be on their mobile phones.

People want to playback all their experiences, by video, mobile phones or tablets, they do not want to take a picture with their brain and store it in their memory banks.

Some people do not grow because they are constantly reminded of their past by media.

Remember when you die you can take anything with you, but your memories. Spend more time outdoors, do a sport. Live now, change now, death is guaranteed and you never know when she will come knocking on your door.

Say no to gangsterism, drugs, violence and crime. Love is an easier emotion to deal with than hate. Think positive.

I am

I can

It is done
I can do it
I can do anything
I believe
Choose love and light always!

"I know what I am planning for you...I have good plans for you, not plans to hurt you. I will give you hope and a good future"
-The Bible; Jeremiah 29.11-

Killer without remorse

Chapter One

Barring a blizzard or something bordering on a hurricane, Noleen always walked to work from her house in Yeoville to her office in Berea. A thirty-four-year-old clinical psychologist, she had a practice and at the same time had established something of a public persona as a host of a radio talk show, 3 talk with Noleen, which aired five days a week for one hour.

The early morning air on this October day was crisp and breezy, and she was glad she had opted for a long sleeve sweater under her suit jacket. Her shoulder length hair still damp from the shower was wind-blown, causing her to regret not wearing a scarf. It was only seven-thirty, and the streets were not crowded yet. In another hour they would be teeming with back-to-work Africans.

Thank heavens the weekend's over, Noleen said to herself. She had spent most of Saturday and Sunday comforting her mother, who had been in low spirits and understandably so, Noleen thought, since Sunday would have been her fortieth wedding anniversary. Then, not helping the situation, Noleen had an unfortunate encounter with her older sister, Tricia, who was visiting from Polokwani.

On Sunday afternoon, before returning home, Noleen had made a courtesy call to her father's palatial home in Port Elizabeth, where he and his second wife, Mia, were throwing a party. Noleen suspected that the timing of the party was Mia's doing. I love my parents, she thought as she reached her office building, but there are times when I want to tell them to grow up.

217

Noleen was usually the first to arrive on the top floor, but as she passed the offices of her old friend and mentor Marcia, she was startled to see the lights in the reception area and hall were already on.

She shook her head ruefully as she opened the outer door – which should have been locked – walked down the hallway, then stopped at the open door leading to Marcia's office.

One of the most respected attorneys in South Africa, Marcia's grandmotherly appearance offered little indication of the cleverness and aggressive energy she brought to her work. The two women had met and become friends ten years ago at Pretoria University, when Noleen was a student and Marcia a guest lecturer.

All of Noleen's friends, Marcia being the exception, had been shocked when after two years in the Durban District Attorney's office, Noleen quit her job as a District Attorney to go back to school to earn her doctorate in psychology. Sensing Noleen's presence in her doorway, Marcia looked up. 'Well look who is here, good weekend Noleen?'

Marcia knew about both Pinky's party and the anniversary. 'It was predictable,' Noleen said. 'Tricia got to mom on Saturday, and the two of them ended up sobbing their hearts out. I told Tricia that her depression was making it harder for mom to cope, and she blasted me, said if I had watched her husband swept to his death in an avalanche the way she watched Glen die then I would understand what she was going through.

'Then there was Dad and Mia's party at the turreted mansion he built for her,' she continued incidentally. 'Dad now requests that I call him James, which says it all on that subject.' She sighed deeply. 'Another weekend like that and I will be the one that needs counselling.'

Marcia eyed her sympathetically. She was the one of Noleen's friends who knew the full story about Tricia and Glen and about Noleen's parents and the messy divorce. 'Sounds to me as if you need a survival plan,' she said.

Noleen laughed. 'Maybe you will come up with one for me, just put it on my tab with all I owe you already as well as the radio and television job. Now I'd better get going. I have to prepare for the show.'

A year earlier Felicia, a popular radio host and a close friend of Marcia's, had invited Noleen to sit in on her programme during a highly published trial to comment both as a legal expert and psychologist. The success of that first day on air led to regular appearances on the programme.

Noleen was asked to replace Felicia when she accepted job offer abroad. 'Who is your guest today,' Marcia asked.

'This week I will be concentrating on why women should be safety conscious in social situations. Vanessa Lewis a psychiatrist specialising in criminology, has written a book Missing Woman. Many of the disappearances were solved, but a number of interesting ones are still open.

'We will discuss why an intelligent woman might get involved with a killer and how listeners might avoid potentially dangerous situations. Good subject, I think so. I've decided to bring up the Rachel Marks disappearance. That one always intrigued me. Remember her, we used to watch her on television and thought she was great.'

Marcia looked up frowning. Rachel Marks had disappeared about two years earlier after disembarking from a train in Welkom. 'I remember it very well. It got a lot of publicity at the time.'

'That was after I left, the attorney offices,' Noleen said, 'but I was visiting a friend there when Rachel's mother Zara who lived in Escourt at the time came in to talk to the director of prosecutions to see if he would help. There was no indication that Rachel had ever left Welkom so Durban had no jurisdiction. The poor woman had photos of Rachel and kept saying how much her daughter had looked forward to that trip, I have never forgotten the case.'

Marcia's expression softened. 'I knew Rachel Marks slightly, we graduated from UNISA the same year. She lived at Bencorrum Mews then. She was always quiet. I gather she was also shy socially.'

Noleen raised her eyebrows. 'I wish I had known. You might have been able to arrange for me to speak to Rachel's mother Zara.'

Marcia frowned. 'Maybe it is not too late, and Russell Gilbert is the Marks family lawyer. I have met him on a few occasions, he lives on City Park Avenue; I will call him at nine and see if he will put us in touch with her.'

At ten past ten the intercom on Noleen's desk buzzed. It was Megaline her secretary. 'Russell Gilbert is on line one.' As soon as Noleen began to speak to the Marks family lawyer, it became clear that he was not happy. 'Noleen we absolutely resent exploitation of Mrs Marks's grief,' he said brusquely. 'Rachel was her only child, it would be bad enough if her body had been found, but because it has not. Mrs Mark's agonises constantly, wondering under what circumstances her daughter may be living, if she is alive. I would have thought that a friend of Marcia's would be above this sensationalism.'

Noleen pursed her lips together for an instant to cut off the heated response she was tempted to make. 'Mr Gilbert you have already given the reason why the case should be discussed. Neither the police nor the investigator Mrs Marks hired was able to uncover a single clue as to what Rachel did or where she might have gone after disembarking.

'My programme is heard nationally , It's a long shot, I know, but maybe someone who is listening today was on that train or was living in the area at the time and will call in to tell us something helpful, after all Rachel was on television regularly, and some people have an excellent memory for faces.'

Without waiting for a response, Noleen hung up, leaned over and turned on the radio. She had made intros and promos for today's programme, referring to her guest author and Rachel's case. They had run briefly last Friday and Hilton, her producer, had promised that the station would air them again this morning. Ten minute later she heard the first promos. Now let's keep our fingers crossed that someone who knows about the case is listening too, she thought.

It was definitely a lucky stroke that his car radio was tuned to the radio station that Friday. Otherwise he would have never heard the announcement. As it was he was barely listening. But at a mention of Rachel Marks's name he turned up the volume and concentrated intently. Not that there was anything to worry about, of course, as always he had taken every precaution.

Now hearing the news again on Monday he was less sure. Next time he would be especially careful. But then the next one would be the last. There had been four so far, one more to go. He would select her next week, and once she was his, his mission would be complete and he would finally be at peace.

Angrily he listened to the warm, encouraging voice of Noleen. 'Rachel Marks was a renowned investment adviser; she was also a daughter, a friend and a generous benefactor of charities. We will be talking about her disappearance on my show today. We would like to solve the mystery. Maybe one of you has a piece of the puzzle, listen in please.'

He snapped off the radio. 'Noleen', he said out loud, 'all this is none of your business, and if I was you, if I have to make you my business, your days are numbered … '

The book non-fiction and ready for publication early 2014.

Reference

Permissions
Numbers 26 27 28, Prison Gang Mythology, by Inga Papp 2007. SERVAMUS community based safety & Security magazine. *www. servamus.co.za*
   Crime statistics; Africa Check, a fact finding website: www. africacheck.org

Further reference
District Six; "Making amends for apartheid: the resurrection of District Six". The Independent. 15 March 2004. "District Six Museum". International Coalition of Historic Sites of Conscience. Western, John. Outcast Cape Town. Berkeley: University of California Press, 1996.
   Bezzoli,Marco; Kruger, Martin and Marks, Rafael. "Texture and Memory The Urbanism of District Six" Cape Town: Cape Technikon,
   Dewani; BBC News. *"South Africa honeymoon murder husband arrested in UK"*, Bristol, 8 December 2010. BBC News. *"Anni Dewani honeymoon murder: South African jailed"*, 8 August 2012. .South African Press Association (5 December 2012). *"Life sentence handed down for Dewani killer"*. Mail and Guardian.
   Sizzlers Murders; Crime library article by Martin Strohm *www. crimelibrary.com*
   Staggie; *"Cape gang leader in court for murder"*. Mail&Guardian Online. 04.09.2007
   Ellis, Estelle 14.11.2000 *"Drug dealer shot and set on fire by vigilantes"*. Independent Newspapers (South Africa).

"Staggie granted day parole". South African Press Association. 21.05.2013

Murder Statistics in South Africa: *www.saps.co.za*

Printed in Great Britain
by Amazon